STAY COOL

IN SCHOOL

C000202970

Text copyright © Margaret Goldthorpe 2003
Illustrations copyright © Jane Taylor 2003
The author asserts the moral right
to be identified as the author of this work

Published by
The Bible Reading Fellowship
First Floor, Elsfield Hall
15–17 Elsfield Way, Oxford OX2 8FG
ISBN 1 84101 323 4

First published 2003
10 9 8 7 6 5 4 3 2 1 0
All rights reserved

Acknowledgments
Unless otherwise stated, scripture quotations are taken from the Contemporary
English Version published by The Bible Societies/HarperCollins Publishers,
copyright © 1991, 1992, 1995 American Bible Society.

Scripture quotations taken from the Holy Bible, New International Version,
copyright © 1973, 1978, 1984 by International Bible Society, are used by
permission of Hodder & Stoughton Limited. All rights reserved. 'NIV' is a
registered trademark of International Bible Society. UK trademark number 1448790.

A catalogue record for this book is available from the British Library

Printed and bound in Malta

STAY COOL
IN SCHOOL

Margaret Goldthorpe

A BIBLICAL APPROACH TO TEACHING MORAL VALUES THROUGH CIRCLE TIME

ACKNOWLEDGMENTS

There are, as usual, so many people to thank! Writing a book is a pretty lonely exercise in many ways but at the same time very dependent on the efforts, goodwill and inspiration of many others.

I should like to thank and acknowledge all the people who have helped and influenced me, but that is impossible! I would be writing these acknowledgments for weeks if I tried to do that. So I shall just have to do my best, and if I offend anyone I can assure them it is a sin of omission, not commission.

I should like to acknowledge two particular churches who have been hugely influential in this book. The first are the Quakers. For many years my Sunday mornings were spent sitting quietly in a Quaker meeting house. It is hard to explain how far one can spiritually travel in the relative silence of a Quaker meeting. I am also thankful to them for all of the books I have read over the years concerning their unique contribution to peace.

I am also indebted to another, startlingly different, church. Since 1999 my family has attended Soul Survivor, Watford. This is a church whose focus is entirely towards young people. It is not a quiet place!. It has, however, not only helped to revolutionize worship music worldwide but also, through its festivals, conferences and publications, helped to bring thousands of young people into a close and personal relationship with Jesus.

I am grateful to Soul Survivor for their inspiration, their prayers and for all I have learned from their teaching. It's from them that I have learned that we should not only try to tell people the good new—we should also try to be good news. This book was an effort to do both, Mike—to do some 'telling' and to do and encourage some 'being'.

I am, as always, indebted to Alexandra School, where I have taught off and on for the last ten years. In particular, thanks to Lindsey for trialling some circle times, to Perdy for the 'Recipe for a good school' and to Chris, Nicki and Charlie for letting me 'practise' these circle times on their classes.

I should also like to thank Jenny Mosley, with whom I have worked for the past ten years, for her circle time inspiration.

There are many authors whose books have greatly influenced me. In particular, I should mention Stephen Covey, John Drane, Philip Yancey, J. John, Steve Chalke, Rob Parsons and M. Scott Peck.

I should also like to thank, sincerely, my ever patient, ever encouraging, ever cheerful editor at BRF, Sue Doggett.

Last, but never least, thanks to my family—my husband Dennis and my four lovely teenaged children. They are always so encouraging and cheerful (and noisy!). They are a blessing indeed!

For further information regarding circle time, INSET and other training for your school, please contact me direct:

Margaret Goldthorpe
'Stay Cool in School'
Midsummer Cottage
Moor Lane
Sarratt
Herts
WD3 6BY
Tel: 01923 262586

CONTENTS

FOREWORD

Many schools struggle with how Religious Education and Personal and Social Education (PSE) can work together without losing the integrity of either of the subjects. In this book, Margaret Goldthorpe has provided a model that schools can use to do just that. Using the *content* of the Sermon on the Mount, she provides Circle Time activities to develop its relevance in the *context* of the pupils' immediate lives (those with a faith and those with none). So this book is a practical manual on developing pupils' skills to reflect on moral values, which also provides them with the tools to be able to apply those values in their lives at school and with friends and family. It is, as Margaret claims, 'a very practical book'.

Margaret combines her extensive knowledge and experience of working with Circle Time with an accessible approach to the moral values contained in the Sermon on the Mount. The result is a flexible structure to enable teachers and pupils to understand the Christian teachings more fully, consider how they can have relevance in our everyday lives and to reflect on our own attitudes and how they affect our behaviour.

Starting with the basic principles of Jesus' teachings, translated into pupil-friendly language and with a summary of 'God's Guidelines', the book provides New Testament stories that illustrate the teaching. These stories are the 'RE' part of the structure, and can be linked to Literacy to develop pupils' skills and understanding. They provide excellent opportunities for exploring character, interpretation and emotions, as well as the power of story as a means of communication. Above all, they enable non-specialist teachers to convey what the Sermon on the Mount can mean to Christians.

The 'RE' part does not stand on its own, however. It is rather a stimulus to lead in to the practical application of the model. Each story has a follow-up Circle Time to help pupils 'learn from' the religious content. Tapping in to her wealth of experience as a teacher and trainer for Circle Time, Margaret has developed flexible activities that engage the pupils in personal reflection on and practical application of the issues explored. From 'Being honest with ourselves' to 'Learning to forgive', pupils are encouraged to plan ways in which they can apply the principles in their lives over the ensuing week. These are then celebrated at the start of the next week's Circle Time to encourage the pupils to 'walk the talk'.

This is all rooted firmly in the pupils' everyday experience in school and elsewhere. As such, this book does not only provide for individual personal development, it also offers schools a structure in which to address the sort of community it wants to create. This is a textbook for effective RE, but it is also much more. It is a manual for whole school values and promoting positive attitudes and behaviour.

And it is fun!

Bill Moore
Senior RE Inspector for Buckinghamshire

'THE GRASS ISN'T GREENER ON THE OTHER SIDE OF THE FENCE;

IT'S GREENER WHERE YOU WATER IT.'

A MODEL FOR RELIGIOUS EDUCATION IN SCHOOLS

This book is designed for use as part of the Key Stage 2 RE syllabus. It aims to give Key Stage 2 children an understanding of the Christian religion through a practical and experiential exploration of the moral and spiritual issues raised in the New Testament Bible, especially the part usually called the Sermon on the Mount. It does not require the children to have Christian beliefs.

It is to help children of all faiths and none to have a real understanding of the way Jesus of Nazareth said we should live.

To this end, the book contains favourite New Testament Bible stories written in modern, child-friendly language. Each story is designed to form the basis of an RE lesson for Key Stage 2 children. It presents the story in its biblical context and gives a brief summary of the meaning of the story.

This is also a very practical book. Each issue raised by a passage from the Sermon on the Mount and further illustrated in the selected stories also has a matching circle time.

In these circles, children are encouraged to consider the moral and ethical implications of Jesus' advice for their own lives.

The circle times are about issues such as how we deal with peer pressure, learn to admit we were wrong, accept apologies gracefully, or handle a desire to show off. The children are asked to think about making plans of action to manage these problems in the light of an increased understanding of their own behaviour. The wisdom from the Sermon on the Mount is on hand to guide them.

This is well expressed in the introduction to the Buckinghamshire Agreed Syllabus for RE 2001:

How we behave affects other people and the world we live in.

↓

This is why our behaviour is an important issue.

↓

Our behaviour is influenced by our attitudes.

↓

Our attitudes are influenced by our beliefs.

We all play a part in creating the world we live in. What we believe, whether religious or not, contributes significantly to this. RE helps pupils, and the school as a whole, to reflect on the ways in which beliefs influence the way people live their lives.
APPENDIX 3 OF *RELIGIOUS EDUCATION IN BUCKINGHAMSHIRE.*
PRODUCED BY BUCKINGHAMSHIRE SACRE.

Victor Frankl, a Jewish psychiatrist who survived the Nazi concentration camps, said this about what enabled him to survive:

Everything can be taken from a man but one thing—the last of the human freedoms—to choose one's attitude in any given situation.

Giving children the tools to make this choice is the purpose of this book.

CHAPTER 1

DANCING TOWARDS THE LIGHT

HELPING EACH OTHER TO BE OUR BEST SELVES

RE is not simply about teaching a narrative or body of knowledge. It is also a subject that helps us to think about how we live our lives. It is a place to discuss ethics and spiritual issues.

If we need emotional literacy, we also need ethical and spiritual literacy.

Christians believe that in the New Testament we have the word of God through the person of Jesus to give guidance and advice about how to live our lives in the best way possible, so that we may be our best selves—the selves God made us to be.

In the Old Testament, this advice was given as clear rules and instructions, with punishments to follow if rules were not kept.

In the New Testament, Jesus gives his followers clear advice, such as the advice given in the Sermon on the Mount. He also helps us to understand his advice by illustrating his teaching with parables and stories of everyday life. They enable us to see how we can apply his teaching to our lives. But Jesus' guidelines, as given in the Sermon on the Mount, are not like rules. They are too hard for that! It is not possible always to love your enemies or turn the other cheek. There are few people in the world who have even nearly managed to live by the teaching of the Sermon on the Mount. Mahatma Gandhi, who was a Hindu, was one of them. But it is very, very hard.

The instructions in the Sermon on the Mount are for the perfect way to live. They are God's guidelines for how we should try to live, but when we fail we are not to punish each other. That is proper for the world's rules and laws, but not for God's. Jesus does not say that God will punish us for failing. He says that God will punish us for not trying. He said that when we fail we are to apologize to God, admit our weakness, ask God for more help and go on trying. The Christian New Testament says that we cannot reach God under our own steam, but as long as we try to live as he wishes us to, then God's grace will help us.

It can help to picture it like this. Imagine God is standing in a golden doorway. He wants us to join him and he is keen for us to pass through the door into the lighted room beyond. In order for us to get there, we need to travel across the room. But we are not to go marching along, bumping into each other, pushing each other over and throwing each other out of the way. Rather we are to travel by following the complicated and difficult steps of a beautiful, graceful dance. This dance, if danced correctly, will help us along. What is more, we won't have hurt each other but rather we will have helped each other, as we travel along together.

But the dance is impossibly difficult for most of us and we continually fall over! God does not mind: he just wants us to get up and keep trying. A few, such as Mahatma Gandhi and Mother Teresa, turn out to be beautiful dancers.

God gave us Jesus to be our dancing teacher: he is the way. God also gave us his Holy Spirit to be our personal coach: he is our helper. God never minds how many times we fall over or how awful we look as we dance, provided we do our very best and we never give up trying. If we won't dance, or we don't try our very best and go our own way instead, that is our choice, but we cannot then expect to find that, somehow, we are the other side of the golden door.

That is why the guidelines are not rules. They are simply about us trying to learn how to follow the Lord of the Dance.

CHAPTER 2

GOD'S GUIDELINES

SOME OF THE TEACHING IN THE SERMON ON THE MOUNT AND ITS SUMMARY

In this book the teaching in the Sermon on the Mount is summarized and called 'God's guidelines'.

It is very important to stress that these guidelines are not in any way designed to be a set of school or class rules. They are not designed to replace any rules you may have in place in your school, although an understanding of the teaching of the Sermon on the Mount may well enhance children's understanding of the rules your school has.

School rules, when broken, incur a sanction, and that's as it should be, but this is not appropriate for 'God's guidelines'. We are not in charge of the sanction system for these rules!

Here is some of the teaching from the Sermon on the Mount:

When Jesus saw the crowds, he went up on the side of a mountain and sat down. Jesus' disciples gathered around him, and he taught them (Matthew 5:1–2).

Treat others as you want them to treat you. This is what the Law and the Prophets are all about (Matthew 7:12).

You know that our ancestors were told, 'Do not murder' and 'A murderer must be brought to trial.' But I promise you that if you are angry with someone, you will have to stand trial (Matthew 5:21–22).

Don't store up treasures on earth! Moths and rust can destroy them, and thieves can break in and steal them. Instead, store up your treasures in heaven, where moths and rust cannot destroy them, and thieves cannot break in and steal them. Your heart will always be where your treasure is (Matthew 6:19–21).

I tell you not to swear by anything when you make a promise! … Say only 'Yes' or 'No'. Anything else comes from the devil (Matthew 5:34, 37).

You can see the speck in your friend's eye, but you don't notice the log in your own eye… Take the log out of your own eye. Then you can see how to take the speck out of your friend's eye (Matthew 7:3, 5).

Good people do good things because of the good in their hearts. Bad people do bad things because of the evil in their hearts. Your words show what is in your heart (Luke 6:45).

God blesses those people whose hearts are pure. They will see him! (Matthew 5:8).

If you forgive others for the wrongs they do to you, your Father in heaven will forgive you. But if you don't forgive others, your Father will not forgive your sins (Matthew 6:14–15).

I tell you to love your enemies and pray for anyone who ill-treats you (Matthew 5:44).

Don't condemn others, and God won't condemn you. God will be as hard on you as you are on others! He will treat you exactly as you treat them (Matthew 7:1–2).

You know that you have been taught, 'An eye for an eye and a tooth for a tooth.' But I tell you not to try to get even with a person who has done something to you. When someone slaps your right cheek, turn and let that person slap your other cheek (Matthew 5:38).

You cannot serve both God and money (Matthew 6:24).

When you do good deeds, don't try to show off. If you do, you won't get a reward from your Father in heaven…When you give to the poor, don't let anyone know about it. Then your gift will be given in secret. Your Father knows what is done in secret, and he will reward you (Matthew 6:1, 3–4).

I tell you not to worry about your life. Don't worry about having something to eat, drink, or wear. Isn't life more than food or clothing? … Only people who don't know God are always worrying about such things. Your Father in heaven knows that you need all these. But more than anything else, put God's work first and do what he wants. Then the other things will be yours as well (Matthew 6:25, 32–33).

Ask, and you will receive. Search, and you will find. Knock, and the door will be opened for you… Would any of you give your hungry child a stone, if the child asked for some bread? Would you give your child a snake if the child asked for a fish? As bad as you are, you still know how to give good gifts to your children. But your heavenly Father is even more ready to give good things to people who ask (Matthew 7:7, 9–11).

Reproduced with permission from *Stay Cool in School* published by BRF 2003 (1 84101 323 4)

Below is a simplified version of the biblical text. Throughout this book, these simplified versions are called 'God's guidelines'.

GOD'S GUIDELINES

Treat other people as you would have them treat you.

*Stay calm, do not be angry with each other, never take revenge
and never try to get your own back or get even.*

Look into your heart and be honest, especially with yourself.

Be loving and forgiving to all people, even to those you really don't like and who don't like you.

Be aware of your own faults but never judge or criticize other people.

*Don't put all your efforts into being rich—you can't take it with you!
Instead, work really hard at being your best self.*

*Don't show off, letting everyone know how good or clever or generous you are.
Instead, go about your life quietly and with humility, trying to do your best.*

*Don't worry too much about what you will wear or what you will eat. The most important
thing is to live as God wants you to live, to ask for his help and trust in his care.*

CHAPTER 3

PLANNING THE LESSONS AND CIRCLE TIMES

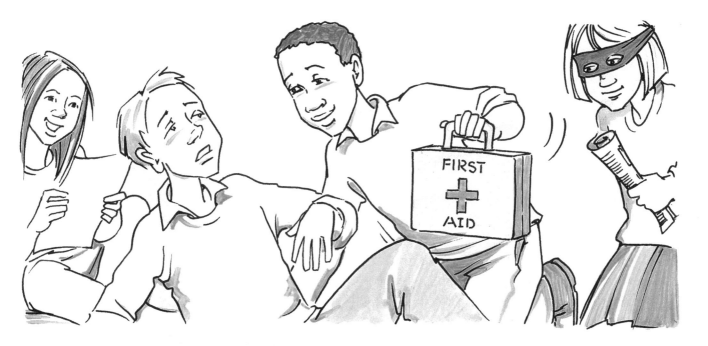

TEMPLATE PLAN OF EACH RE LESSON AND CIRCLE TIME

The teaching of the Sermon on the Mount is not easy. It is hard to see how we can even begin to live such a perfect life! I suggest that the only way even to start is to:

- Read the stories and parables that Jesus gave us to illustrate his teaching.
- Honestly explore how this teaching applies to us in our own lives.
- Work out exactly which part of the Sermon on the Mount we should be trying to be guided by.
- Find a way of living that follows those guidelines.
- Keep a track of how we are doing.

Each of the lesson plans in this book therefore starts with part of the teaching from the Sermon on the Mount, followed by a New Testament story taken directly from the Contemporary English Version of the Bible and then retold as a paraphrase. For your RE lesson, you can read the Bible story just as it is written (in either version) to the whole class. You can then choose to let the children take parts and act it out, as a class or in groups, using puppets, masks, dance, music or mime.

You may wish to read the story at the beginning of circle time, but it is far better to do it as a separate RE lesson. Reading the story, ensuring that the children have taken it in, and then going on to do a circle time, all in the same lesson, will either take too long or lead to a superficial understanding of these complex issues. Also, taking time to act out the story, or make it into a puppet play, is good fun. Rushing it through would destroy this element of enjoyment.

So, after the story comes a matching circle time plan to help children to address personally the issues in the story. I strongly recommend that you read through the story and the entire circle time plan, consider the needs of your class, then transfer parts of the plan on to the blank, photocopiable, circle-planning sheets provided on pages 20–21.

Although you don't have to read the plan as a script, it is important to stick to the basic format of the circle time lesson as it follows a particular problem-solving sequence. In the Old Testament, King Solomon asks God for help. He realizes that, as a king, he needs to know what he should do when things are going wrong. God gives this reply: 'If my people, who are called by my name, will humble themselves and pray and seek my face and turn from their wicked ways, then will I hear from heaven and will forgive their sin and will heal their land' (2 Chronicles 7:11–14, NIV).

Expressed in more secular terms, this means that if we have decided we want to sort out our problems, we must first say, 'I don't think I'm quite on the right lines here. What is more, I need to be honest with myself and *get real* about where I might possibly be going wrong' (that is, 'humble ourselves').

Then we need to stop and think seriously about what we should be doing, saying to ourselves, 'Help! What should I do here? Maybe it won't be the easy thing, but I need to know the right thing to do. We need to *get right* with each other, looking to God's guidelines and thinking about what is the right thing to do' (that is, 'pray and seek God's face').

Lastly, we need to think, 'In that case we had better *get together* with each other and come up with a plan, a way forward. If we are to improve the situation, we need to come up with some suggestions of things we could do instead, that will get us on to the right path' (that is, 'turn from our wicked ways').

This is how the circle times in this book are organized—structured around a plan first given by God to Solomon three thousand years ago, using advice given by Jesus of Nazareth two thousand years ago. It's an old plan, but still, I believe, the best way of sorting out problems.

Given below is the outline structure of each RE lesson and circle time, to show how it works in practice.

RE LESSON PLAN

Each lesson is headed by some teaching from the Sermon on the Mount, with a summary of this teaching in the form of 'God's guideline'. After this

there is a story from the New Testament, which has been chosen to illustrate the teaching point from the Sermon on the Mount, followed by an explanation and a retelling of the same story in child-friendly language.

This week's Bible story

Read, discuss and explore the Bible story during your RE lesson in as many ways as you can invent. In order to develop the story further and deepen the children's understanding of the story, you could try:

- Using puppets or shadow puppets
- Acting out the story
- Retelling the story in a modern context
- Music or mime
- Role play
- Painting scenes from the story
- Making textile pictures

CIRCLE TIME PLAN

Begin with an attitude of gratitude

Start by being thankful for all of the good things that have come out of the previous week's circle time. Use this time to refer to, and critically review, successes recorded on the circle time noticeboard, to particular children and any successes they may have had, and for any other good outcomes. If necessary, critically discuss any failures. Jot comments down in the space provided on the circle time planning sheet.

There is no point in creating a plan to help us live as our best selves if we do not check that we have put the plans into action. One danger of circle time is that the children know all the right things to say, but have no intention of actually putting themselves out to change their behaviour over a period of time. Looking at the noticeboard, reviewing successes, and having a brief discussion can help to encourage the children to 'walk the talk'.

Bible story summary

A summary of the Bible story comes next in each circle time plan. You may not need this: it will depend upon the time lapse between the circle time and the preceding RE lesson.

Get started

This section introduces the week's topic, following on from the story read in RE. The games or activities are specifically designed to help the child to feel and personally experience something of the issue under discussion, but they are also designed to be good fun. Make a note of games played on the photocopied circle time planning sheet.

Get real

This section is where we start to think honestly and with humility about how the theme of the Bible story applies to us. Usually we will go around the circle hearing from each child. Use a guiding 'I' sentence as you go round the circle. For example, if we were looking at the story of the prodigal son and the nature of forgiveness, then we might use a sentence

that starts, 'When I say "sorry" it helps if I…'

Whenever you have a 'go-around', remember to use a conch or 'speaking object'. This just means that you pass an object around the circle as the children speak. Only the person who has the conch can speak. No one else is allowed to speak when the conch holder is speaking. This ensures that everyone has their own uninterrupted time to be heard.

This section is not always done immediately as a whole class 'go around'. Sometimes the children break into groups for a brief discussion and then come back to the circle.

Get right

Summarize the children's responses to the 'Get real' section. Then ask them to think back to their RE lesson and the teaching from the Sermon on the Mount. What did Jesus say we should do in the situation under discussion? Which of God's guidelines is relevant to this circle time?

For example, in the case of the prodigal son the guideline is, 'Be loving and forgiving to others (even those you don't get along with)'. The lesson, after all, was also to the prodigal's brother. He had to learn to forgive as his father had forgiven.

Never forget—'God's guidelines' are not rules!

Get together

Now you explore the theme further, asking the children to work together to find a way to apply this new understanding to their own lives in school. Ask, 'If that's what Jesus wants us to do, how can we do it? How can we change our attitudes or behaviour?' Ask the children to suggest how they can plan ways to move forward, using God's guidelines to help them to be their best selves. Try to construct a plan with targets. I have included suggestions and ideas with each circle time in case your class is stuck. You don't have to use any of them but you might find them helpful.

If you are recording the lesson using the photo-copiable planning sheet, jot the class's ideas down here.

Keep going (This week's noticeboard)

Over the years I have run hundreds of circle times. For the most part they have been very satisfactory, but I have found one or two recurrent problems. One problem is the difficulty some classes have in maintaining and sustaining the good intentions they have expressed in circle time. During circle time, the children may be genuinely concerned about an issue, and they may come up with some splendid suggestions for putting a problem right. But three days later you might find that they have lapsed somewhat into their old ways! I have found that creating and using an RE circle time noticeboard helps to keep the class focused on their ambitions.

First of all, you need a real noticeboard. You may already have one on the wall or you might have to construct one. I would suggest a size of about 120cm wide and 90cm high (4ft x 3ft). Use ordinary pinboard with a wooden frame. You can use this noticeboard to record and display the plans the children create during their RE circle times.

Each circle time in this book has a noticeboard activity which aims to keep children focused on their good intentions for the whole of the week following

the circle time. It may also help children to gain a clearer understanding of the often complex spiritual, ethical or even theological concepts in the Bible stories. At the beginning of the next circle time you can have a brief chat about the successes of the previous week as shown on the noticeboard. You may wish to have a longer discussion of the noticeboard at some other time in the week. You might want to develop the ideas further at other times. You might, for example, wish to use some of your ideas for assembly.

Use your noticeboard in the classroom to do some of the following:

- Use the ideas generated by your class.
- Use the ideas put forward in this book.
- Record the successes the class has had in putting their plans into action.
- Make photographic displays of children putting their ideas from circle time into action.
- Display material from outside the school which has helped the children further to understand the RE lesson (for example, information from world aid organizations such as Oxfam, Save the Children, World Vision).
- Celebrate success from assemblies following on from RE lessons.

Using the noticeboard needs a great deal of initial planning but once it is sorted out you will (I hope!) get years of use from it.

Keep it in mind

This 'saying of the week' will also go on the noticeboard. It is designed to act as a kind of jingle to remind the class of how they are trying to be their best selves during the week. For example, the 'saying of the week' for the prodigal son is, 'Friendship is for giving.'

The saying of the week concludes the circle time.

CHAPTER FOUR

ASSESSMENT, RECORD KEEPING, AND THE VALUE OF A DIGITAL CAMERA

A BLANK PHOTOCOPIABLE CIRCLE PLANNER

Several times in this book I will suggest using a digital camera, usually to record children putting their circle time suggestions into practice. This will enable them to see themselves 'walking the talk'. If you are fortunate enough to have such a camera, you could also take photographs of the noticeboard for each lesson.

We live in an age of obsessive record keeping and assessment, both of teachers and pupils. It can be helpful to keep a track of which issues you have tackled both in RE and in circle time and, most importantly, what the children actually learned from these sessions.

I would suggest that you keep a file containing:

- Records of your RE lessons.
- The circle time planning sheets filled in with the children's subsequent responses, ideas and suggestions for plans of action.
- A photograph of the noticeboard recording and monitoring their plans.
- A photographic record of how the children put these plans and ideas into action in their own lives.
- Comments recorded on the 'attitude of gratitude' section, concerning their feeling of success or otherwise.

This record should satisfy the most exacting demands of OFSTED, threshold and performance management.

If teachers find records of circle times useful, so do the children. I have seen several good examples of class circle time books that teachers have made, containing all of the good ideas their classes have had during their circle times.

One example was from Gayhurst Primary School in Hackney. Here, the class teacher would record all the good ideas the children had during the circle time for solving their problems and being their best selves. She then typed them up and gave each child a copy, which they kept in a file in their trays. Should anyone in the class, or indeed the whole class, meet a similar problem or face a similar difficulty at any other time in the year, they could consult their book.

The advantage to this was that they did not have to keep having circle times about the same problems. The teacher could say, 'When we talked about this in circle time we came up with some good ideas. We tried some of them at the time. We are now facing similar problems again. Let's look in our books and try another of the ideas we had.'

My colleague, Lucy Nutt, used a similar idea. However, instead of each child having their own book, she had one large class circle time book in which she kept all of the ideas generated by her class.

CIRCLE PLANNER AND RECORD KEEPING SHEET

RE LESSON

Bible story _____

_____

_____

_____

CIRCLE TIME

Begin with an attitude of gratitude _____

_____

_____

_____

_____

Bible story summary _____

_____

_____

Get started (Ice-breaker) _____

_____

_____

_____

_____

_____

_____

_____

_____

_____

_____

_____

_____

Reproduced with permission from *Stay Cool in School* published by BRF 2003 (1 84101 323 4)

(!) **Get real (The 'go-around' sentence)** _____

_____

_____

(✓) **Get right (What would Jesus want us to do?) Which guideline is relevant here?**

_____

_____

(☺) **Get together (Discuss the issues and plan a way forward)** _____

_____

_____

_____

_____

_____

_____

_____

_____

_____

_____

_____

(→) **Keep going (This week's noticeboard)** _____

_____

_____

_____

_____

_____

_____

_____

_____

_____

_____

_____

_____

_____

_____

(☁) **Keep it in mind (Saying of the week)** _____

_____

_____

Reproduced with permission from _Stay Cool in School_ published by BRF 2003 (1 84101 323 4)

VINEYARDS AND SKATE PARKS

WHY WE NEED THE SERMON ON THE MOUNT

Jesus of Nazareth lived two thousand years ago. Christians believe he is God's son. They believe he came from God to teach people. They needed this teaching so that they could work out how to live in such a way that they would please God. Christians also believe that Jesus died to save everyone from their sins and pave the way for us to be able to have a relationship with God for ever.

This was not God's first effort at teaching people directly. In the Old Testament, God gave his prophet Moses ten very special laws. These are called the Ten Commandments. They are:

1. Do not worship any god except me.
2. Do not make idols that look like anything in the sky or on earth or in the sea under the earth.
3. Do not misuse my name.
4. Remember that the Sabbath day belongs to me.
5. Respect your father and mother.
6. Do not murder.
7. Be faithful in marriage.
8. Do not steal.
9. Do not tell lies about others.
10. Do not want to take anything that belongs to someone else.

These were rules, and there were punishments if you broke these rules. They are still a really important set of rules, and they are still really difficult for us to keep!

When Jesus came, many years later, he said that he had not come to change a word of these rules. He said he had come to give them their full meaning, and he added the 'new commandment' that we should love one another as we love ourselves. He taught people how to live in such a way that God would be pleased with them and would welcome them into heaven to live with him for ever. Christians believe he came to show us how we might be our best selves—the people God wants us to be, the people God made us to be.

Jesus taught these things throughout his life, but there was one very special day when he gave a great deal of teaching all at one time. That teaching is known as the Sermon on the Mount. This is some of what he said on that special day:

When Jesus saw the crowds, he went up on the side of a mountain and sat down. Jesus' disciples gathered around him, and he taught them (Matthew 5:1–2).

Treat others as you want them to treat you. This is what the Law and the Prophets are all about (Matthew 7:12).

You know that our ancestors were told, 'Do not murder' and 'A murderer must be brought to trial.' But I promise you that if you are angry with someone, you will have to stand trial (Matthew 5:21–22).

Don't store up treasures on earth! Moths and rust can destroy them, and thieves can break in and steal them. Instead, store up your treasures in heaven, where moths and rust cannot destroy them, and thieves cannot break in and steal them. Your heart will always be where your treasure is (Matthew 6:19–21).

I tell you not to swear by anything when you make a promise! … Say only 'Yes' or 'No'. Anything else comes from the devil (Matthew 5:34, 37).

You can see the speck in your friend's eye, but you don't notice the log in your own eye… Take the log out of your own eye. Then you can see how to take the speck out of your friend's eye (Matthew 7:3, 5).

Good people do good things because of the good in their hearts. Bad people do bad things because of the evil in their hearts. Your words show what is in your heart (Luke 6:45).

God blesses those people whose hearts are pure. They will see him! (Matthew 5:8).

If you forgive others for the wrongs they do to you, your Father in heaven will forgive you. But if you don't forgive others, your Father will not forgive your sins (Matthew 6:14–15).

I tell you to love your enemies and pray for anyone who ill-treats you (Matthew 5:44).

Don't condemn others, and God won't condemn you. God will be as hard on you as you are on others! He will treat you exactly as you treat them (Matthew 7:1–2).

You know that you have been taught, 'An eye for an eye and a tooth for a tooth.' But I tell you not to try to get even with a person who has done something to you. When someone slaps your right cheek, turn and let that person slap your other cheek (Matthew 5:38).

You cannot serve both God and money (Matthew 6:24).

When you do good deeds, don't try to show off. If you do, you won't get a reward from your Father in heaven…When you give to the poor, don't let anyone know about it. Then your gift will be given in secret. Your Father knows what is done in secret, and he will reward you (Matthew 6:1, 3–4).

I tell you not to worry about your life. Don't worry about having something to eat, drink, or wear. Isn't life more than food or clothing? … Only people who don't know God are always worrying about such things. Your Father in heaven knows that you need all these. But more than anything else, put God's work first and do what he wants. Then the other things will be yours as well (Matthew 6:25, 32–33).

Ask, and you will receive. Search, and you will find. Knock, and the door will be opened for you… Would any of you give your hungry child a stone, if the child asked for some bread? Would you give your child a snake if the child asked for a fish? As bad as you are, you still know how to give good gifts to your children. But your heavenly Father is even more ready to give good things to people who ask (Matthew 7:7, 9–11).

Reproduced with permission from *Stay Cool in School* published by BRF 2003 (1 84101 323 4)

Phew! This is very complicated language but, put simply, it means this:

GOD'S GUIDELINES

Treat other people as you would have them treat you.

*Stay calm, do not be angry with each other, never take revenge
and never try to get your own back or get even.*

Look into your heart and be honest, especially with yourself.

Be loving and forgiving to all people, even to those you really don't like and who don't like you.

Be aware of your own faults but never judge or criticize other people.

*Don't put all your efforts into being rich—you can't take it with you!
Instead, work really hard at being your best self.*

*Don't show off, letting everyone know how good or clever or generous you are.
Instead, go about your life quietly and with humility, trying to do your best.*

*Don't worry too much about what you will wear or what you will eat. The most important
thing is to live as God wants you to live, to ask for his help and trust in his care.*

In this book, these are called 'God's guidelines'. They are not rules in the same way that the Ten Commandments are rules. For example, although the last guidleline says that you shouldn't worry too much about your food or your clothes, you won't be punished if you sometimes get into a state about what you are going to wear to the school Christmas disco! The guideline about not worrying over your clothes means that you have to get your priorities right. You should worry much more about doing the right thing than about your clothes.

Jesus said that we should put all our efforts into living God's way. If we fail, and get it wrong, he said we should try doing this:

1. Be honest with ourselves about what we have done wrong.
2. Say sorry to God.
3. Try very hard indeed not to do it again. If we do get it wrong again, start back at 1.

Jesus told people stories to illustrate these guidelines. In these stories he talks about ordinary people and their problems and difficulties. He gives them advice about how they should live so that they can please God.

The problem for us is that Jesus lived two thousand years ago by a big lake in the Palestine countryside.

This means that ordinary people to him were fishermen, shepherds, Roman soldiers, temple priests and people who owned vineyards. That is not very ordinary to us, and sometimes it can make Jesus' teaching seem a bit remote from our lives. It also makes it all sound rather difficult and complicated. It doesn't help that some Bibles are in very old and very odd language.

But try to think of it this way: Jesus just talked about the ordinary people he lived among and their everyday problems, and he talked in very ordinary language. If he were alive today, he wouldn't tell stories about vineyards, shepherds, fishermen and wineskins. No, he would tell stories about shopping centres, plumbers, van drivers and Macdonalds. Instead of gardens, sheep, lepers, wine, bread-making, Pharisees and Samaritans, he'd talk about skate parks, football grounds, cars, people with AIDS, Coca Cola, fast food, pompous politicians and asylum seekers.

Our scenery might look different from first-century Palestine, but the people and their problems are just the same. We are all still just trying to do the best we can in a difficult world. In those days, people had problems that are no different to ours. They lost their temper, wanted each other's stuff and talked about each other behind their backs. They also worried about having no friends, or had to listen to people showing off about how clever they are. All the things that bother us bothered them. Jesus came to tell us that God understands this and that he has sent Jesus to help us, to show us how we can live with each other and be our best selves. God is still the same too—and he still loves us!

AND THE TRUTH WILL SET YOU FREE

> God blesses those people whose hearts are pure. They will see him!
>
> MATTHEW 5:8

○ ○ ● GOD'S GUIDELINE ● ○ ○

Look into your heart and be honest, especially with yourself.

THE PARABLE OF THE TWO SONS

Jesus said: I will tell you a story about a man who had two sons. Then you can tell me what you think. The father went to the elder son and said, 'Go and work in the vineyard today!' His son told him that he would not do it, but later he changed his mind and went. The man then told his younger son to go and work in the vineyard. The boy said he would, but he didn't go. Which one of the sons obeyed his father?

'The elder one,' the chief priests and leaders answered.

Then Jesus told them, '…When John the Baptist showed you how to do right, you would not believe him. But these evil people did believe. And even when you saw what they did, you still would not change your minds and believe.'

MATTHEW 21:28–32

Jesus knew that it was very important for us to learn to be honest people. But being honest can be really difficult. We know we must not tell lies, not even little itty-bitty ones. We also know that we must not take each other's money or things, even when we convince ourselves we are only borrowing them. But Jesus said that there is much more to being honest than this. You also have to be able to be truly honest with yourself.

Jesus used to get really cross with people who lied to themselves—especially people who were so proud that they could not be honest with themselves and admit when they were wrong. But you have to be very brave to be so honest with yourself that you can face an uncomfortable truth about yourself.

Jesus once had a problem with the chief priests of the temple. These people would not believe Jesus when he said he had God's authority to teach God's wishes for how people should live. They did not want to believe Jesus. They knew that if they did believe him, they would have to change their minds and admit they had been wrong—and to admit you are wrong can be very hard. But if we are to be our best selves, we must be able to say, 'I am going to have a change of heart, because I was wrong.' Jesus explained it like this.

There was once a man who had two sons. This man needed the boys to help him at work. He said to the eldest son, 'Could you give me a hand at work today, son?' This boy said, 'No, I don't want to.' But later he knew that he had been wrong to say that, so he changed his mind and he went and helped his father. The man also asked the second son if he would help him. The second son said, 'Sure, Dad, I'll help you.' But when it came to it, he didn't turn up.

Jesus said to the chief priests, 'Who do you think the father was most pleased with?'

'Easy,' said the priests. 'The first son.'

'You're right,' said Jesus. 'But you lot are like the second son. You say, "Oh, yes. We'll do it, we'll follow God's word." But when someone showed up to teach you God's word, you wouldn't listen to him. And now, you won't admit you were wrong, change your mind and listen to me. It would be better if you could be like the first son. If you were like him, you could admit you got it wrong in the beginning. Then, you could change your minds, do the right thing and follow the teaching I am giving you.'

This did not endear Jesus to the chief priests. They did not like being criticized. They did not want to have to face the truth that maybe they had been wrong. They started to plot to have him arrested.

BIBLE STORY SUMMARY

The two sons

In the story of the two sons, Jesus talks about being honest with yourself. He told the story of a man and his two sons. The man asked the first son to help him, but the boy said, 'No, I don't want to.' But then he was honest with himself, knew he had done the wrong thing and went and helped his father.

The second son said, 'Oh sure, Dad. I'll help.' But then he didn't bother to turn up. Jesus says that if, like the first son, you have chosen to do the wrong thing, then you must be honest with yourself about your behaviour, change your mind and do the right thing. The point of this story for us is that it is very important that we are honest with ourselves, that we recognize when we have done something wrong and that we change our minds and do the right thing.

GET STARTED

Traffic lights

Ask all the children to stand in the middle of the circle. Explain that you are going to ask them what they would do as part of a group in various scenarios. Your left-hand side of the circle is 'red light'. This is the side for 'No'. Your right-hand side of the circle is 'green light'. This is the side for 'Yes'.

Read out each of the scenarios from pages 28–30. The children must decide on their response and run to the 'red light' or 'green light' on the word 'Go'.

If you have time after playing the game, you could put the class into groups of about six pupils each. Have the scenario cards on pages 28–30 photocopied before the lesson, and give one card to each group. Ask them to act out the scenario, perhaps once with one ending and then with a different ending.

TRAFFIC LIGHTS SCENARIO

You are the class clown! Everyone thinks you are really funny and a total laugh. But your mum is on your case about SATS. You think that maybe you should stop mucking around and do a bit of work. If you do, people will wonder what has happened to you. Also, they might stop laughing at your jokes! Do you change?

⬤ RED?　　⬤ GREEN?　　⬤ GO! ━━━▶

Reproduced with permission from *Stay Cool in School* published by BRF 2003 (1 84101 323 4)

TRAFFIC LIGHTS SCENARIO

You are part of the 'popular' group in your year. A new boy comes to the school. Your group decides he is 'sad' and they won't have anything to do with him, so you ignore him. After a while you can tell he is really lonely, but you know that if you befriend him you will be thrown out of the popular group. Do you change your mind, make friends with him and risk being rejected by the group?

 RED?   GREEN?    GO!

TRAFFIC LIGHTS SCENARIO

You can't find your purse. You and your friends are sure that a girl in your class has stolen it. You spend ages discussing the problem and bad-mouthing the girl you suspect. Every time you see her, you give her 'the evils'. Your group has even started to whisper to other people in the year about your suspicions. Eventually your whole group, full of righteous anger, decides to tell the teacher. While you are all on the way to see the teacher, you find your purse. You stop everyone from going to the teacher. *But*—do you say to the group that you should all go back and apologize to the girl?

RED?   GREEN?   GO!

Reproduced with permission from *Stay Cool in School* published by BRF 2003 (1 84101 323 4)

TRAFFIC LIGHTS SCENARIO

Your class has a part-time science teacher every Tuesday afternoon. She is a bit hopeless and everyone messes her around really badly. One day you stay behind after class to help clear up and you get talking to her. You realize she is a very nice person. Suddenly you feel really bad about your behaviour in her lesson. You want to change and try hard for her. If you do change, your group will call you a 'creep' or a 'suck-up' or a 'boff'. Do you change?

 RED?   GREEN?    GO!

TRAFFIC LIGHTS SCENARIO

You take up a new activity outside school (like music lessons, drama classes, ballet, church, or a new football or rugby team). None of your friends in school knows about it. The group of children you meet there are really different from your friends in school. They wear different clothes, like different music, watch different television programmes, everything! You like the outside school group a great deal. In fact, you have decided they are probably much, much nicer than your school group. When you are with them you know you are a nicer person.

Non-uniform day is tomorrow. You know that if you wear the clothes that you wear with your outside school friends, everyone will know that you have changed. If you wear the same clothes as your school group, it stays a secret. Do you wear your outside school clothes and show everyone you have changed and become a slightly different person?

 RED?   GREEN?    GO!

Reproduced with permission from *Stay Cool in School* published by BRF 2003 (1 84101 323 4)

GET REAL

Go around the circle using the sentence, 'It is really hard to admit you were wrong and change because…'

Give everyone twenty seconds' thinking time before you go around the circle.

GET RIGHT

Summarize the children's responses to the 'Get real' section. What would Jesus want us to do? He would want us to look into our hearts, be honest with ourselves and do the right thing.

We can't do the right thing if we are not honest with ourselves first. Even if that means admitting we have been wrong or done something wrong, Jesus says, 'God blesses those people whose hearts are pure. They will see him! (Matthew 5:8).

So which of God's guidelines is relevant to this circle time?

> Look into your heart and be honest, especially with yourself.

Jesus is saying, 'Don't lie to yourself. Be honest with yourself, if necessary have a change of heart and then act accordingly.'

GET TOGETHER

Have a discussion about the scenarios. Talk about why it is so hard to be honest with yourself. Discuss the difficulties of peer pressure, isolation, the fear of being shunned, laughed at or left 'best-friendless'.

How can we do the right thing, knowing how important it is to learn to look into our own heart, be honest with ourselves and have a change of heart if necessary? How can we begin to act in the way we now know is right? Encourage the children to think of how they might be able to change their behaviour and maybe even be different from their peers. Take each 'traffic lights' scenario card and ask them how they could begin to address the issues with their friends. Perhaps they could think of some opening lines they might use:

- 'I've been thinking, and I've decided to…'
- 'I was thinking last night about what happened yesterday, and I think I will…'
- 'I am not saying this is the only thing to do, but I think I will…'

Write down all the ideas they have.

KEEP GOING

KEEP IT IN MIND

This week's noticeboard

If possible, make two 'photostories' of one of the scenarios. Using a digital camera if you have one, or a regular camera if not, take a series of photographs, one of each scene of the story. (If you are unsure what a photostory looks like ask a pupil to bring in a popular girls' magazine—they are full of them!) Ask the children to act out the stories and take 'stills' of each scene.

Cut the photographs out and mount the photostories on the noticeboard. You might want to use two different colour backing papers—red and green —to show clearly which story involves someone having a change of heart and acting upon it, and which one shows them concealing their change of heart.

Saying of the week

Sometimes a healthy heart is a change of heart!

or

Remember, it's one thing to talk the talk but we also have to learn to walk the talk!

DON'T WORRY, BE HAPPY, 'COS EVERY LITTLE THING'S GONNA BE ALL RIGHT

I tell you not to worry about your life. Don't worry about having something to eat, drink, or wear. Isn't life more than food or clothing? … Put God's work first and do what he wants. Then the other things will be yours as well.

MATTHEW 6:25, 33

Ask, and you will receive. Search, and you will find. Knock, and the door will be opened for you… Would any of you give your hungry child a stone, if the child asked for some bread? Would you give your child a snake if the child asked for a fish? As bad as you are, you still know how to give good gifts to your children. But your heavenly Father is even more ready to give good things to people who ask.

MATTHEW 7:7, 9–11

‑‑ ∘○● GOD'S GUIDELINE ●○∘ ‑‑

Don't worry too much about what you will wear or what you will eat. The most important thing is to live as God wants you to live, to ask for his help and trust in his care.

‑‑ ∘○● ✝ ●○∘ ‑‑

THE PARABLE OF THE FRIEND AT MIDNIGHT

When Jesus had finished praying, one of his disciples said to him, 'Lord, teach us to pray, just as John taught his followers to pray.'

So Jesus told them, 'Pray in this way:

Father, help us to honour your name.
Come and set up your kingdom.
Give us each day the food we need.
Forgive our sins,
as we forgive everyone who has done wrong to us.
And keep us from being tempted.'

Then Jesus went on to say: Suppose one of you goes to a friend in the middle of the night and says, 'Let me borrow three loaves of bread. A friend of mine has dropped in, and I don't have a thing for him to eat.' And suppose your friend answers, 'Don't bother me! The door is bolted, and my children and I are in bed. I cannot get up to give you something.'

He may not get up and give you the bread, just because you are his friend. But he will get up and give you as much as you need, simply because you are not ashamed to keep on asking.

So I tell you to ask and you will receive, search and you will find, knock and the door will be opened for you. Everyone who asks will receive, everyone who searches will find, and the door will be opened for everyone who knocks.

LUKE 11:1–10

Have you ever watched someone doing something quite skilled, like playing football or the guitar, or painting or singing, and thought, 'I wish I could do that as well as they can'? Well, the disciples used to

watch and listen to Jesus praying and they noticed that his prayers seemed to work—they got answered. When Jesus prayed for blind people to see and lame ones to walk, he got results! The disciples felt that their prayer skills were nowhere near as good as those of Jesus, so the disciples tackled him about his prayer

technique. Next time the subject came up, they said to Jesus, 'Lord, teach us to pray.' First of all, Jesus gave them a very important prayer that they could say every day. We call this the Lord's Prayer. It went like this:

Father, help us to honour your name.
Come and set up your kingdom.
Give us each day the food we need.
Forgive our sins,
as we forgive everyone who has done wrong to us.
And keep us from being tempted.

He then taught them how to pray in a way that would please God. He had already told them, when he preached his Sermon on the Mount, that they were not to pray in a showy way but should go into a room and pray quietly to God. Now he also told them that they mattered to God and so they should natter to God. The disciples still looked doubtful. This wasn't how they were used to seeing people pray. They were used to seeing the Pharisees standing in the temple and making a big noisy show of their prayers. The disciples were worried. Would all this quietly-sitting-in-your-room-having-a-chat-to-God business really work?

Jesus looked at them. He could see that he would have to explain it in a way they could more easily understand.

'I'll tell you what,' Jesus said. 'Try thinking of it like this. Suppose some friends unexpectedly turn up very late one night to visit you. Although you are thrilled to see them, you have no food in the house, as you planned to go shopping the next day. So you rush round to your next-door neighbour's house and bang on their door. Eventually they open a bedroom window.

'"What on earth is going on?" they say. "It's the middle of the night!"

'"I am so sorry," you say, "but some friends have turned up unexpectedly and they are starving hungry and I haven't got a thing in the house to give them. Could you lend me some bread and milk and eggs? I am so sorry to bother you."

'Your neighbour is not pleased and you have to do a fair amount of pleading, but eventually he gets up to help you and gives you some bread and milk and eggs!

'Now,' said Jesus to the disciples, 'if someone who

Now you are not often short of food at midnight! How can we understand this matter of asking God for help?

It's a bit like this. You are growing up at the moment and trying to become the best person you can be, but sometimes you need some help. Maybe you have been impatient with your little brother or sister and wish you hadn't. Perhaps this makes you wish you had more patience. Where are you going to get this patience?

Jesus said that you can pray to God and ask him and he will give it to you. You might have to keep praying but eventually you will get more patience.

Jesus said that you just sit quietly and ask God. You say, 'Dear Lord, thank you for all the things you have already given me, and I'm sorry about the way I am not always my best self. At the moment I am being a bit impatient with my little sister. I wish I wasn't. Please could you help me be more patient?'

Keep asking and you will get the help you need.

You can't pray for just anything. You can't pray for money, fame or power. They tend to be sourced from a different supplier! But you can pray for things such as love, joy, peace, patience, kindness, goodness, faithfulness, humility and self-control. You can also pray for help, guidance and protection. Jesus says these are the kind of things that, if you keep asking, you will be given.

is only a neighbour would eventually help you, imagine what God—who loves you dearly and is your heavenly father—would do for you! You just have to keep asking. You see, if you pray persistently, God will help you. If you ask God for help you will be given it, and if you knock on God's door he will definitely open it to you. But you must ask.'

The disciples smiled at each other. They understood much more now. Pray persistently and with faith. They could do that!

So they thanked Jesus and went away to practise.

BEGIN WITH AN ATTITUDE OF GRATITUDE

Start by being thankful for all the good things that came out of last week's circle time. Use this time to refer to, and critically review, successes recorded on the noticeboard. Refer to particular children and any successes they may have had, and note any other good outcomes from last week's circle time.

BIBLE STORY SUMMARY

The friend at midnight

In this week's story we learned how Jesus taught the disciples to pray. He told them that they had to pray persistently and know that their prayers would be answered. He also said that God is generous and loving and wants to look after people.

Jesus said that prayers can be made up by anyone.

You don't have to find them in a book, or be a vicar, or be rich or old. Lots of Christian children have a helpful way of writing their own prayers. They remember the abbreviation for 'teaspoon' in cookery books—**tsp**. Then they say **t**hank you to God for all of the blessings they have received, **s**orry for the things they have done wrong, and **p**lease when they ask God for help, guidance or protection.

GET STARTED

Trust train

Move a few chairs away from the circle so that there are 'holes' in the circle.

Put the children into teams of five, and ask each team to stand in a queue. Now ask the children to put their hands on the shoulders of the person in front of them. Explain that they are a train. The person at the back is the driver; the person at the front is the engine. The engine will go where the driver tells it to go.

If the driver taps with their left hand on the left

shoulder of the person in front of them, that person has to pass the tap along to the next person, and so on down the line to the engine—who turns left.

Passing down a right-hand tap on the right shoulder turns the engine right. Passing down a tap on both shoulders means 'go straight on'. Passing down a gentle pull on both the shoulders, with both hands, means the engine stops. There is no reverse!

Get everybody to practise tapping and passing along the taps really efficiently. Then tell everybody that their trains are now about to set off around the room—but there is one further instruction. Everybody, apart from the driver at the back, must have their eyes tightly closed. This is scary for the engine at the front. This is why the game is called 'Trust train'!

At the end of the game, explain that Christians believe that God knows each one of us individually. They also believe that he loves each one of us dearly, and that if we put our trust in him he will keep us safe. If we ask him for his help, he will be better at guiding us around than we can be!

GET REAL

Show the children a mobile phone, and ask them to imagine they are going to ring up their mum, dad or whoever is their chief carer. You can describe how the phone doesn't have wires but it enables you to speak straight into the mind of your dad or whoever.

Then explain that Christians believe praying is like this. There are no wires, but you talk straight to God. It's as easy as that. You just have to imagine that you don't have a 'cell' phone but a 'soul' phone. God's soul phone is never switched off!

Christians believe that God made the world and us. Jesus says we should try to live according to the maker's instructions, and if we have problems, we should phone the helpline! God will then guide us in the right direction.

Use a go-around sentence: 'If I could use the soul phone and get some help it would be for…'

GET RIGHT

In the Bible story, Jesus said that people were not to try to do everything under their own steam. He said that God is like the best father imaginable, and we are to trust him. He will take care of us if we pray and ask for his help.

So which of God's guidelines is relevant to this circle?

> Don't worry too much about what you will wear or what you will eat. The most important thing is to live as God wants you to live, to ask for his help and trust in his care.

When you have a problem, pray and ask for God's help and trust that he will help you. We should try to learn to live by trusting God, not always thinking we can do it all by ourselves. God has a good view of the big picture. We should learn to trust him.

GET TOGETHER

Usually in circle time we think about how we can alter our own lives for the better, by our own efforts. This circle time is quite different. Christian prayer is about trust in God. Therefore, for the children to understand this concept, they need to supply the 'thank you's, 'sorry's and 'please's, but not the answers!

Go around the circle putting the children into groups of three, labelling the children a, b, c, a, b, c, and so on. Ask the 'a's to think of something the class could be thankful for, the 'b's something they could say sorry for, and the 'c's something they could ask for help, guidance or protection for. The can share their answers with the two others in their group. Put them back in the circle and get all the 'a's to swap places, then all the 'b's to swap places, then all the 'c's. In their new group, ask them to tell each other their ideas and to write these ideas down.

KEEP GOING

This week's noticeboard

Cut out mobile phone shapes, using the photocopiable template opposite.

Ask the groups to write their thank you, sorry or please ('tsp') prayers on the phones, and decorate them as they choose. Pin the phones up on the noticeboard.

How you use these prayers is up to you. If you are teaching in a Church of England primary school, you may want to use them in assembly or have children read them out in class as prayers at the beginning and end of the school day. You may even want to discuss at the beginning of the next circle time how some of the prayers have been answered, and say thank you. If that is not appropriate in your school, you may simply wish to label the noticeboard, 'These are some examples of Christian prayers.'

It is quite likely that some children will ask to write their prayer in text message language. Why not let them? It could be fun, and God will understand text language! The only thing to stress is that, however they write the prayers, they must understand that prayer is a serious business and not to be mocked.

KEEP IT IN MIND

Saying of the week

I'll get by with a little help from my Friend!

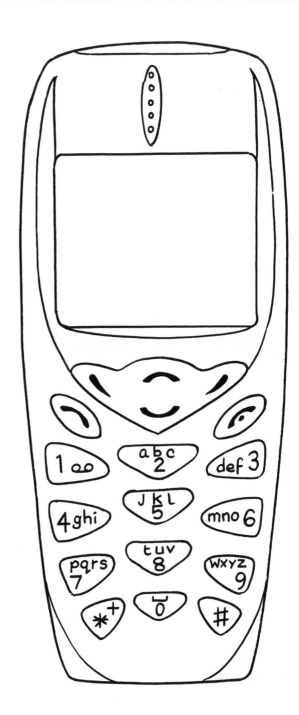

Reproduced with permission from *Stay Cool in School* published by BRF 2003 (1 84101 323 4)

TEN THINGS I LIKE ABOUT YOU

> Treat others as you want them to treat you. This is what the Law and the Prophets are all about.
>
> MATTHEW 7:12

—∘ ○ ● **GOD'S GUIDELINE** ● ○ ∘—

Treat other people as you would have them treat you.

—∘ ○ ●  ● ○ ∘—

THE PARABLE OF THE SHEEP AND THE GOATS

When the Son of Man comes in his glory with all his angels, he will sit on his royal throne. The people of all nations will be brought before him, and he will separate them, as shepherds separate their sheep from their goats.

He will place the sheep on his right and the goats on his left. Then the king will say to those on his right, 'My father has blessed you! Come and receive the kingdom that was prepared for you before the world was created. When I was hungry, you gave me something to eat, and when I was thirsty, you gave me something to drink. When I was a stranger, you welcomed me, and when I was naked, you gave me clothes to wear. When I was sick, you took care of me, and when I was in jail, you visited me.'

Then the ones who pleased the Lord will ask, 'When did we give you something to eat or drink? When did we welcome you as a stranger or give you clothes to wear or visit you while you were sick or in jail?'

The king will answer, 'Whenever you did it for any of my people, no matter how unimportant they seemed, you did it for me.'

Then the king will say to those on his left, 'Get away from me! You are under God's curse. Go into the everlasting fire prepared for the devil and his angels! I was hungry, but you did not give me anything to eat, and I was thirsty, but you did not give me anything to drink. I was a stranger, but you did not welcome me, and I was naked, but you did not give me any clothes to wear. I was sick and in jail, but you did not take care of me.'

Then the people will ask, 'Lord, when did we fail to help you when you were hungry or thirsty or a stranger or naked or sick or in jail?' The king will say to them, 'Whenever you failed to help any of my people, no matter how unimportant they seemed, you failed to do it for me.'

Then Jesus said, 'Those people will be punished for ever. But the ones who pleased God will have eternal life.'

MATTHEW 25:31–46

Not all of the stories Jesus told had happy endings. Lots of the stories were serious warnings to people. One day, while he was sitting up on a hill called the Mount of Olives, Jesus told his disciples that although we live on this earth and think we are in charge of it, God is really in charge. One day we will have to answer to God as to how well we lived on this earth. Did we listen to his advice about how to live as our best selves, the people he meant us to be? Or did we just do as we liked, with no thought for others?

It is a bit like us when the teacher is out of the room! The teacher says, 'I am leaving you here on your own for a little while. You know how to behave, so be your best selves and I will be proud of you when I get back. If I find you messing around when I get back, there will be trouble. Don't say I haven't warned you!'

But sometimes we are not our best selves, and while the teacher is out of the room we are silly. Some people shout out and make a din; others interfere with those who are trying to be good and stop them working. Still others are actually nasty and tease people and are unkind. The longer the teacher is away, the worse things get. The room becomes a mess and no work gets done. The noise is awful and some children are crying because of the teasing and unkindness. Eventually the teacher comes back in and everyone goes quiet. They are ashamed.

Look at the room and their behaviour! The teacher

is furious. Quickly she gets everyone quiet. Then she points to all those children who are out of their seats or are all red because they have been racing around. She also points to those who are making others cry or are teasing them, and she says, 'Right! You and you and you,' pointing at the naughty ones, 'over here. The rest of you can go out to play.' Then she keeps the naughty ones in and says they can have no playtime and no treats. They must stay in and scrub

the desks, including getting the chewing gum off from underneath. They also have to scrub the dining tables and chairs and go around the playground picking up the mess and the litter, while the children who tried to be good are allowed to play. She says to the naughty ones, 'I trusted you to be good, but you betrayed my trust. I have told you many times how you should behave but when you thought I was not looking you just did as you liked. Well now you must suffer your punishment. I warned you what would happen. You have brought this on yourselves.'

Jesus told his disciples that there would be a day like this for everyone. He called it 'Judgment Day'. On the Mount of Olives he explained it like this.

On Judgment Day, God's king will come with his angels. He will sit on a magnificent throne and he will call all of the people of the earth before him. Then he will point to them and say, 'You go to the right, you to the left.' He will separate them out like a shepherd separates sheep from goats (just like the returning teacher separated the naughty children from the good ones).

All the good people will sit by the king's right hand. And he will say to them, 'Come, you can go into the kingdom that was prepared for you at the beginning of time' (just like the children who were their best selves were allowed to go out to play). 'For when I was hungry you fed me, when I was thirsty you gave me a drink, when I came as a stranger you made me welcome. When I had no clothes you found some for me, when I was sick you cared for me and even when I was in prison you visited me and comforted me.'

Then all the people will look at each other in amazement and say, 'When did we do this?' The king will say, 'When you did one of these good and kind things for even the least of my people, you did it for me.'

Then the king will turn to those on his left side and say, 'But you, you can get out of my presence. You will receive nothing good' (just as the naughty children will have to miss playtime and do horrid chores). 'When I was hungry you just let me starve, when I was thirsty you let me go without water, when I was a stranger in your land you rejected me. You let me wear rags, you did not care for me when I was sick and you abandoned me when I was in prison.'

The bad people will say, 'When did we ever do this to you?' The king will say, 'Whenever you did these bad things to even the poorest of my people, you did it to me. Now get away from me and go into the darkness for ever.'

Jesus told the people on the Mount of Olives that he was giving them a warning. He said he was not joking—we must be our best selves. We will be held to account, just like we are in school.

BEGIN WITH AN ATTITUDE OF GRATITUDE

Start by being thankful for all the good things that came out of last week's circle time. Use this time to refer to, and critically review, successes recorded on the noticeboard. Refer to particular children and any successes they may have had, and note any other good outcomes from last week's circle time.

BIBLE STORY SUMMARY

The sheep and the goats

This is a story about the grave importance of being our best selves. Jesus said that we would have to answer for our behaviour one day. He also said that we should not just be nice to people we know or people who are important. We should be our best selves towards everyone, all the time, everywhere. He said we were to:

- Feed hungry people
- Give water to thirsty people

- Care for people we are just getting to know
- Find clothes for poor people
- Care for sick people
- Remember people in prison

Explain that today we are going to think about caring for people we are just getting to know. The people we are thinking about are the children who are new to our school. This is primarily going to be Reception year pupils, but the ideas are applicable to children who may enter the school at any time. The ideas may be especially helpful for children who come from refugee families and will be in urgent need of as many friends as possible.

GET STARTED

Getting to know you

Sit all the children in the circle and explain to them that they must follow your instructions:

- All stand up and generally mill around the circle. (This must be done in silence.)
- Stop.
- Say hello to everyone you pass.
- Walk.
- Stop.
- Give a 'high five' to the next six people you pass.
- Walk.
- Stop.
- Make a group of four.
- Ask each other the question, 'If you could invite anyone into this room, who would it be?'
- Split up and mill around the room again in silence.
- Make a group of three.
- Tell each other about the last time you can remember being scared.
- Walk.
- Stop.
- Turn to the person next to you.
- Label yourselves 'A' and 'B'.

- Tell each other which piece of music or song always makes you feel cheerful.
- 'B' close your eyes tight.
- 'A' take 'B's hand and lead them back to a chair in the circle. Carefully shield them from any harm as you lead them back.
- Sit down next to them.

GET REAL

Go around the circle using the sentence, 'My first memory of this school is…'

GET RIGHT

Summarize the children's responses to the 'Get real' section. Explain that on your first day you are:

- New—a stranger to the place
- Young
- Missing your mum
- Scared of the big kids (and that's just the year 2s!)
- Lost in a strange, big place
- Small

Maybe you joined the school in a year other than Reception and you had problems such as finding a friend, feeling different, missing your old best friend.

What would Jesus want us to do? In the Bible story, he said, 'Whatever you do for even the least important person, you do for me.'

So which of God's guidelines is relevant to this circle?

> **Treat other people as you would have them treat you.**

GET TOGETHER

Encourage a discussion about the difficulties we all feel when we are new to any situation.

Ask the children to think of ways in which they might help new children to feel better when they first arrive. How might they help a new child to feel welcome? What can we do to ensure that those children will have good memories of their first day in school?

The children should have lots of ideas. Write them all down as they emerge.

Here is a system, called 'Buddies and Pals', that can be used to put all of their ideas into action.

We all need someone who is on our side—someone who looks out for us, comforts us and is there for us when we need a hand or a hug. In the 'Buddies and Pals' system, year 6 children provide that support for Reception year children, intensively for the first week, and just as a close friend for the rest of the year. (You can run this activity with any year group or at any time of year as an imaginary scenario.)

At the end of year 5, each child writes a letter to a specific Reception child who is due to enter the school in September. At the top of the letter there is a digital photograph of the year 5 child. Below that they write something along the lines of:

Dear…

Hello, my name is… I am in class…

I am your Buddy and you are my Pal! I will be there every morning for the first week, as you come to school. I will say hello to you as you say goodbye to the person who has brought you to school. I will walk alongside you to the classroom and then I will say goodbye, but I will be back at breaktime and together we can go out to the playground. If you want, I will stay with you all through break for the first week. There will be lots of other Buddies and their Pals out there, boys and girls, and we can all play together. We know lots of good games that we can teach you. Or we can just sit on the rubber-backed carpet squares and chat. I will also be there for you at lunchtime for the first week.

Six Buddies will be in your classroom to help all of you with your coats, shoes and book bags, morning and evening, for the first two weeks. We do this on a rota, so sometimes it will be me! At the end of the week I will still be your Buddy. We will often see each other at clubs that we will run for you. But remember, if ever you are worried or sad or lonely, come and find me, for until I leave this school I am your Buddy and you are my Pal.

Your friend,

…………………………………

Send a copy of this letter to the parents or guardians of the child who is coming to school. Have another copy ready to give the child when they arrive in school, in case the first was lost or went unread. The second copy is to be taken home, but the Buddy can read it to his or her Pal on the first day, at break or lunchtime.

Here are some ideas to make your 'Buddies and Pals' system successful. You can add the children's own ideas to this list.

• Have badges made for the Buddies and Pals, showing both of their photographs. Encourage both to wear their badges for the first week. This way, any teacher can locate a Buddy for an anxious Pal.

• Be sure you have some rubber-backed carpet squares available for the Infants' playground. This way, Buddies and Pals can sit, chat, play quiet games, look at books together, and play with Duplo, bricks, cars or dolls. It's worth asking several local carpet shops for old samples they could give you.

• Buddies can run indoor lunchtime clubs for the Pals once a week, on a rota basis, for the whole of the winter term. You would probably have to limit the clubs to a maximum of eight or ten children, including about three or four Buddies each time. Only the Reception children who want to go need turn up. Lots would be happy outside playing, but some might like something a little quieter indoors. Each Buddy would probably only have to help at one or, at most, two clubs. The clubs could have a few simple infant party-type games, some play-group songs and maybe a simple story at each session. The Reception children would probably be the best people to teach the year 6s the songs, games and stories.

- Other events could also run at lunchtimes. It is sometimes possible to beg, borrow or buy (at boot sales, for example) small two-wheeler bicycles. The Buddies could teach the non-riders how to ride a bike.

- Buddies who are really good at reading aloud could read favourite stories on to blank tapes for the Pals to listen to in class. It can help a non-reader's progress to follow a story in a book while listening to it on a tape.

Charities

An alternative circle discussion could centre around finding out about the work of different charities which have been set up to meet the needs of the hungry, the poor, refugees and so on—charities such as World Vision, TearFund, Oxfam, Barnardos, or Help the Aged.

However, while the work of these groups is vital, this book aims to give children an experiential understanding of the demands of the Sermon on the Mount. Giving money to charities is very important, but it is also important to learn that is not enough just to give money and then feel better about social injustice of any kind. We also have to learn to live in such a way that, as we grow up, we would not feel happy with ourselves if we did not feed the hungry or care for refugees. Find ways to encourage children to have a social conscience and to see themselves as people who know how to take direct, positive social action.

KEEP GOING

This week's noticeboard

Use the noticeboard this week for children to display ideas for the Buddies and Pals system. They can also display model letters. Get the whole system worked out before putting it into action. *But don't fail to act!*

KEEP IT IN MIND

Saying of the week

> The greatest oak was once a little nut that fell on good ground.

SORRY SEEMS TO BE THE HARDEST WORD

> If you forgive others for the wrongs they do to you, your Father in heaven will forgive you. But if you don't forgive others, your Father will not forgive your sins.'
>
> MATTHEW 6:14

GOD'S GUIDELINE

Be loving and forgiving to all people, even to those you really don't like and who don't like you.

THE PARABLE OF THE PRODIGAL SON

Jesus also told them another story:

Once a man had two sons. The younger son said to his father, 'Give me my share of the property.' So the father divided his property between his two sons.

Not long after that, the younger son packed up everything he owned and left for a foreign country, where he wasted all his money in wild living. He had spent everything, when a bad famine spread through that whole land. Soon he had nothing to eat.

He went to work for a man in that country, and the man sent him out to take care of his pigs. He would have been glad to eat what the pigs were eating, but no one gave him a thing.

Finally, he came to his senses and said, 'My father's workers have plenty to eat, and here I am, starving to death! I will go to my father and say to him, "Father, I have sinned against God in heaven and against you. I am no longer good enough to be called your son. Treat me like one of your workers."'

The younger son got up and started back to his father. But when he was still a long way off, his father saw him and felt sorry for him. He ran to his son and hugged and kissed him.

The son said, 'Father, I have sinned against God in heaven and against you. I am no longer good enough to be called your son.'

But his father said to the servants, 'Hurry and bring the best clothes and put them on him. Give him a ring for his finger and sandals for his feet. Get the best calf and prepare it, so we can eat and celebrate. This son of mine was dead, but has now come back to life. He was lost and has now been found.' And they began to celebrate.

The elder son had been out in the field. But when he came near the house, he heard the music and dancing. So he called one of the servants over and asked, 'What's going on here?'

The servant answered, 'Your brother has come home safe and sound, and your father ordered us to kill the best calf.' The elder brother got so angry that he would not even go into the house.

His father came out and begged him to go in. But he said to his father, 'For years I have worked for you like a slave and have always obeyed you. But you have never even given me a little goat, so that I could give a dinner for my friends. This other son of yours wasted your money… And now that he has come home, you ordered the best calf to be killed for a feast.'

His father replied, 'My son, you are always with me, and everything I have is yours. But we should be glad and celebrate! Your brother was dead, but he is now alive. He was lost and has now been found.'

LUKE 15:11–32

Jesus was not only a healer and a teacher. He was also a fantastic storyteller. This was one of the reasons why he always had great crowds of people following him. People just loved listening to his stories. But these stories always had a very serious point. Jesus didn't ever tell a story just to entertain the crowds; the stories always had an important message.

One of his most famous stories is about a young man who left home and lived a wild life, and then wanted to come back home. This story is often called the parable of the prodigal son, but we can think of it as the story of the boy who behaved very badly, but then came back home and said 'sorry'. The story went like this:

There was once a dad who had two sons. One of them was really good and helpful. The other was a waste of space. He even had the nerve to ask his dad for his inheritance money before his dad had even died! What was worse, he didn't want it for anything good, like buying a house or setting up a business. No, he wanted it so that he could go abroad and live a wild life! But he got his way, and, taking his inheritance money, he travelled abroad and spent all of the money on drink, parties and girlfriends, until in the end he was broke. He had wasted everything his father had given him. In order not to starve to death,

he took a job cleaning out pigs, but he was still so poor that all he had to eat was the bits of food the pigs left.

Then one day he sat down among the pigs and he thought, 'This is the pits. Everybody at home has a better life than me. Even the man who looks after my dad's pigs has a better life than me. I am going home. I will say to my dad, "I am so sorry. I have been awful. Please let me come home. I will work hard for you and I don't even expect to be treated like your son any more. I will live and work just like one of the servants. But please, Dad, just let me come home."'

So the son set off back home to his father. But what he didn't know was that his dad had missed him so desperately that he had watched the road for him every day—longing to see his son again, hoping that every day would be the day he saw him coming home. And then it happened. The father looked down the road as usual—and there was his son!

The father was so happy, he didn't care that he was supposed to behave like the dignified wealthy man he was. He just ran! He ran down the road towards his son, and when he got to him he gave him such a big hug! His son immediately apologized. 'I am so sorry, I have sinned against you and against heaven. I am not worthy to be called your son any more. From now on, treat me like a servant, but please can I come home?'

However, his father just said, 'Quick, get my son some good clothes and some shoes. And give him one of my signet rings to show everyone he belongs to me! Oh, and get the servants to start cooking a celebration meal. Invite everyone! For my son who was lost has been found. Let's have a fantastic party!'

Now the other son, the one who had stayed at home, been a good son, worked hard for his dad and never given him any trouble, was very cross. 'I can't believe this,' he said. 'I've worked so hard for you and never given you a moment's trouble, but you've never thrown a party like this for me and my friends. But my brother, who clears off with your money and then wastes it all on drink and women, he gets a party. It's not fair!'

'Look,' said his father, 'you know everything I have is yours, and you know I love you. But I had lost your brother, he had disappeared, and it broke my heart. Now he's back and I couldn't be happier. Of course I want to celebrate. It's wonderful to have him home. It doesn't mean I love you any less.'

Jesus told this story to show people how much God loves everyone. In the story, God is the father and we are like the son who goes away. Sometimes we get things wrong and behave really badly, but if we go back to God, say sorry and ask for his forgiveness, he will welcome us back with wide open arms. He is just waiting for us to go back and say sorry. It's never too late to say sorry and we have never been too bad to be forgiven by God.

But we also have to take a lesson from the prodigal son's brother. He had to learn to forgive as well. His father showed him how to forgive unreservedly.

BEGIN WITH AN ATTITUDE OF GRATITUDE

Start by being thankful for all the good things that came out of last week's circle time. Use this time to refer to, and critically review, successes recorded on the noticeboard. Refer to particular children and any successes they may have had, and note any other good outcomes from last week's circle time.

BIBLE STORY SUMMARY

The prodigal son (or the boy who came home)
This week's story was about a boy who had behaved really badly. He had run off with the money his dad had given him, he'd squandered it all on drink and loose living, and he'd hit rock bottom. He needed to be rescued. So he came back home, humbly said sorry, asked forgiveness and said he wanted only to be regarded as a servant from now on.

But his father was so happy that he had given up his wicked ways and come home, he welcomed him back as a son and completely forgave him. He even threw a party to celebrate his return. Jesus said that this story was really about our relationship with God. He is like the father and we are sometimes like the bad son. We get things wrong and behave really badly, but Jesus said that if we go back to God, say sorry and ask for his forgiveness, he will welcome us back with wide open arms. He is just waiting for us to go back and say sorry. It's never too late to say sorry and we have never been too bad to be forgiven by God.

Sometimes we need to say sorry to people as well as to God. If God will always forgive us, surely we should learn to ask forgiveness from each other and be forgiving. This can be tough, because people are not perfect like God. Sometimes, when we say sorry to people, they are not kind and they won't accept our apologies—a bit like the prodigal son's brother. We have to learn to accept apologies and forgive people even when we don't get on with them. Sometimes we just find it too hard to say sorry. So saying sorry can be difficult.

But if we don't learn how to say sorry and accept apologies, we can get stuck in miserable situations, full of bad moods, bad behaviour, sulking or grumpiness. In this circle time we are going to think about how we can learn to apologize and accept apologies.

GET STARTED

Play a quick cross-the-circle mixing up game. Cross the circle if you have ever:

- Upset anyone (that should be everyone!)
- Thought 'I'm not going to be the first to say sorry'.
- Found it hard to think how to say sorry.
- Been mean to someone who is trying to say sorry.
- Said sorry and then spoiled it by saying 'But...' as in 'I am sorry I called you a wally, but you shouldn't have said my shoes were naff yesterday.'

GET REAL

Use the template provided below to make a spinner. Photocopy the spinner on to card, and push a spent matchstick, or a craft matchstick, through the centre.

Go around the circle counting the children off into groups of four or five. Let the groups move their chairs into small circles. Give each group a spinner. Ask the groups to use the spinner as a 'conch'. Passing it around the group, each child takes their turn to spin the spinner and finish the sentence provided by the spinner.

Appoint someone from each group to write down their group's suggestions.

After five minutes or so, when you feel that each member of each group has had a chance to speak, recall the groups to the big circle.

Ask if anyone heard something in their group that they thought was interesting. There is no need for them to say who said it. After each contribution, thank the speaker. Take about seven or eight ideas.

Summarize the things that make it difficult to apologize and accept apologies, and those that make it easier.

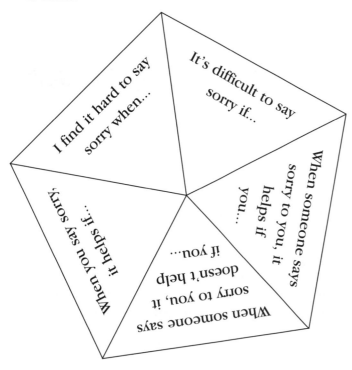

GET RIGHT

What would Jesus want us to do? In the Bible story he said that we can always say sorry to God, and God will always forgive us. If God will always forgive us, surely we should try to learn to do the same. We should learn to ask forgiveness from each other and learn to be forgiving.

Which of God's guidelines is there to help us?

> **Be loving and forgiving to all people, even to those you really don't like and who don't like you.**

○ ○ ○  ○ ○ ○

GET TOGETHER

Encourage a general discussion about the difficulties of apologizing and accepting apologies.

Construct a plan with targets. Using the suggestions from the circle, compile a list of things that facilitate forgiveness and the giving and accepting of apolo-gies. Suggestions might include:

When you say sorry it helps if you…
• Don't plan to do the same thing again.
• Look as if you are sorry.
• Don't laugh and giggle.

Reproduced with permission from *Stay Cool in School* published by BRF 2003 (1 84101 323 4)

- Don't say, 'Sorry but…'
- Don't say 'Sorr-eee' in a way that really means 'I am not sorry at all'.
- Try to think of something you can do to make the situation better, or even make amends.

When someone says sorry to you it helps if you…
- Smile and accept the apology.
- Change the activity to one where you find it easier to be friends.
- Talk normally to the person without looking like you did them a massive favour by accepting their apology!
- Don't gossip about the whole thing behind their back.
- Don't store the whole thing up in your memory so that you can drag it out and use it against them later.
- Say, 'Never mind, let's forget about it and be friends.' Then forget about it and be friends!

If the father in the story of the prodigal son wanted to have a record of the events in his story, I suspect that he would just have had a huge display of happy pictures from the homecoming party. Therefore, my suggestion would be to have blown-up copies of the spinners in the middle of the board. Leading from the segments could be the children's circle time suggestions for apologizing and accepting apologies. Around the edge of the board could be digital pictures taken throughout the week of children happily playing and working together.

If you do not have a camera, you could ask the children to write flashcard-type sentences, outlining events where children have co-operated throughout the week. For example, 'George and Ryan made a model together in art' or 'Louise, Hannah and Laura played with the hamster'. Pin these sentences around the spinners on the noticeboard. In other words, celebrate the children being able to co-operate and be friends, getting along together without arguing and blaming. You could put the 'Saying of the week' as a banner headline across the top of the noticeboard.

KEEP GOING

This week's noticeboard

This can be a difficult subject to display on a noticeboard. You don't want to record instances of children doing silly things and needing to apologize. Neither do you want to record instances of children being 'noble' by accepting apologies.

KEEP IT IN MIND

Saying of the week

Friendship is for giving.

HE'S NOT HEAVY, HE'S MY BROTHER

God blesses those people who are merciful. They will be treated with mercy!

MATTHEW 5:7

- ○ ● ● **GOD'S GUIDELINE** ● ● ○ -

Treat other people as you would have them treat you.

THE PARABLE OF THE GOOD SAMARITAN

An expert in the Law of Moses stood up and asked Jesus a question to see what he would say. 'Teacher,' he asked, 'what must I do to have eternal life?'

Jesus answered, 'What is written in the Scriptures? How do you understand them?'

The man replied, 'The Scriptures say, "Love the Lord your God with all your heart, soul, strength, and mind." They also say, "Love your neighbours as much as you love yourself."'

Jesus said, 'You have given the right answer. If you do this you will have eternal life.'

But the man wanted to show that he knew what he was talking about. So he asked Jesus, 'Who are my neighbours?' Jesus replied:

As a man was going down from Jerusalem to Jericho, robbers attacked him and grabbed everything he had. They beat him up and ran off, leaving him half dead.

A priest happened to be going down the same road. But when he saw the man, he walked by on the other side. Later a temple helper came to the same place. But when he saw the man who had been beaten up, he also went by on the other side.

A man from Samaria then came travelling along that road. When he saw the man, he felt sorry for him and went over to him. He treated his wounds with olive oil and wine and bandaged them. Then he put him on his own donkey and took him to an inn, where he took care of him. The next morning he gave the innkeeper two silver coins and said, 'Please take care of the man. If you spend more than this on him, I will pay you when I return.'

Then Jesus asked, 'Which one of these three people was a real neighbour to the man who was beaten up by robbers?'

The teacher answered, 'The one who showed pity.'

Jesus said, 'Go and do the same!'

LUKE 10:25–37

I am sure you have noticed how easy it is to be nice to people who are nice to us, and how difficult it is to be nice to people who are horrible to us. We just don't want to be nice to people we don't like. That's natural. Unfortunately, though, it's also wrong.

One day, one of the teachers of the scriptures came and asked Jesus the question, 'What must I do to please God and get to heaven?' Jesus looked at the man and answered, 'What do the Scriptures say?' The man replied, 'I have to love God with all my heart and mind and strength, and love my neighbour.'

'Well,' said Jesus, 'that is what you had better do.'

'That's all very well,' said the man, 'but who is my neighbour?' Jesus looked steadily at the man. He felt very sad. By asking, 'Who is my neighbour?' he was also asking 'Who is not my neighbour?' That's a bit like saying, 'I know that in order to go to heaven I have to be nice to a certain group of people. Can we please sort out who exactly they are? That way, I won't have to waste time on the wrong people.' That was definitely not going to please Jesus. However, he did not tell the man off. Instead he told him a story.

One day a man was travelling from Jericho to Jerusalem. Suddenly, he was jumped on by a gang of robbers. They mugged him and beat him up. Then they ran away and left him for dead. As the poor man lay dying by the side of the road, various people came along the same road. The first was a temple priest. He saw the man bleeding and dying and he thought to himself, 'What shall I do? If I help him and he dies, I shall have a problem. I am a temple priest. I'm not supposed to touch dead people. I think I'll just walk on by.'

The next was a Levite. This meant that he was from a very upper-class priestly tribe. He also looked at the poor dying man. He thought, 'I don't like this situation—it looks dangerous. I don't want to get involved. I think I'll just cross the road and pretend I haven't seen him.'

The third person to come along was a Samaritan. (It's very important to know that the Jewish people looked down on the Samaritans.) This Samaritan saw the poor dying man and his heart went out to him.

He quickly went up to him and cleaned up his wounds and bandaged them. Then he carefully put the man on to his mule and took him to an inn, where he took care of him. The next day, he gave the innkeeper two silver coins. 'Please look after him,' he said to the innkeeper. 'I will be back soon and I will repay you whatever else you spend on him.'

'Now,' said Jesus, 'which one of these three acted like a neighbour?' 'The Samaritan,' said the man. 'That's right,' said Jesus. 'Now you go and do the same.'

The man had asked Jesus, 'Who is my neighbour?' Jesus was telling the people that it was wrong to ask, 'Who is my neighbour?' because if you ask that, you are really asking, 'Who is *not* my neighbour? And that's like saying, 'Who *don't* I have to be kind to?'

Jesus was telling the man that everyone is our neighbour—not just our friends and not just people it is safe to be friends with. Neither are we to be fair-weather friends (that means being kind to people only when it's easy and convenient to be kind). We have to be kind to people even when it's awkward, difficult or inconvenient, or even when we don't especially want to be kind. The Samaritan knew this.

The Jews despised the Samaritans. Nevertheless, the Samaritan was very kind to the Jewish man. He knew that it was right to be good to all people, even those who despise you. He knew that every man alive is his neighbour. Jesus said that we are all to be like the Samaritan. Like the good Samaritan, we have to know that everyone is our neighbour. We should love everyone as we love ourselves.

BEGIN WITH AN ATTITUDE OF GRATITUDE

Start by being thankful for all the good things that came out of last week's circle time. Use this time to refer to, and critically review, successes recorded on the noticeboard. Refer to particular children and any successes they may have had, and note any other good outcomes from last week's circle time.

BIBLE STORY SUMMARY

The good Samaritan

Jesus was asked by a teacher of the law, 'Who is my neighbour?' Jesus told this story to show him. The story was about a man who was beaten up and left for dead. He was helped by a kind man from Samaria, even though the Samaritan knew that the beaten man probably despised him. The Samaritan was kind, while the man's own countrymen were so self-absorbed that they abandoned him. It is the story of a Samaritan who knew that every person on the planet is your neighbour. Jesus wanted us to know that all of us belong to each other.

favourite lessons, food and so on. After this, you go around the circle and each child introduces their partner with the words, 'This is my friend… (name) … and we both…'. Each person in the pair says one of the things they both have in common. For example:

Richard: 'This is my friend Rachael and we both like watching *The Simpsons*.'

Rachael: 'This is my friend Richard and we both like holidays in Swanage.'

This activity helps us to see that we have more things in common with each other than we may have previously realized.

GET STARTED

Play a quick cross-the-circle game to mix the children up. For example, say, 'Cross the circle if you have blue eyes… have a J in your name… own a cat…' and so on.

Then play 'Common ground'. To play this, you need to go around the circle putting the children into pairs.

Then give them one-and-a-half minutes to talk to each other. They have to find two things they have in common—for example, hobbies, holidays, pets,

GET REAL

Go round the circle using the sentence, 'I think it's difficult to talk to children I don't know because…'

GET RIGHT

What would Jesus want us to do? In the Bible story, he said that we have to love our neighbour as ourselves and recognize that we are all each other's neighbours.

Which of God's guidelines is relevant to this circle?

> **Treat other people as you would have them treat you.**

GET TOGETHER

We don't have to wait until we find someone half-dead and bleeding by the side of the road before we think about befriending them! We just have to recognize that we all belong to each other.

Encourage a discussion about the difficulties of talking to people who are not in your friendship group.

How can we learn to mix with other 'groups' in our class? Ask the children for ways in which they can counter the difficulties of talking to children they do not know. Write these ideas down.

In the story, the Samaritan was a good neighbour to someone from a different tribe. What is more, these were two groups who hated each other.

Breaching these divides is the first step to seeing that 'everyone is my neighbour'.

Sometimes we label other children in such a way that we almost make them into opposing tribes. There are 'the fat kids tribe', 'the rough kids tribe', 'the sad kids tribe', 'the thick kids tribe', 'the geeky kids tribe', 'the swotty tribe', 'the tarty girls tribe', 'the skaters tribe', 'the hip hop tribe', 'the garage music tribe', 'the townies tribe'—or even 'the ballet girls tribe', 'the horsey girls tribe', 'the Gareth Gates tribe', and so on.

Although it's fine to have preferences, we have to see that we can't denigrate or be nasty to children who are different from us.

See how many different tribes you can think of, and write them down. Don't have any negative tribes—no 'sad' or 'fat' tribes! Some examples of tribes might be might be:

- Types of music—for example, pop, garage, hip hop, indie, rock
- Types of clothes—for example, baseball cap wearers, baggy jeans fans, crop top wearers (or any other current fashion)
- Favourite TV programmes—for example, watchers of *Sabrina*, *Neighbours*, *The Simpsons*
- Favourite lessons
- Favourite bands
- Favourite activities—for example, skateboarding, team games, dancing, gymnastics, football, swimming
- Hobbies—for example, candle-making, Brownies, warhammer, Cubs

As different 'tribes' are mentioned, children who do not like a particular example may well say 'Eugh' or 'They're sad'. Explain that this is the point of the exercise—we are trying to learn to find connections, not exploit differences.

KEEP GOING

This week's noticeboard

Choose about six different 'tribes', such as swimming, types of music, out-of-school activities and so on, which will appeal to both boys and girls. (For example, when I did this with a group of year 6 children we had one category called 'uniformed groups' which included cubs, scouts, Brownies, Guides, Boys Brigade, cadets and so on.)

Now ask the children to make posters, preferably on A3 paper. However, be aware that this will need more space than you have on the circle time

noticeboard alone, and you will need to use other noticeboard space in the classroom.

The posters should have a 'tribe' heading at the top—for example, 'PlayStation Professionals' or 'Simpson's Squad', 'Dance Divas', 'Swimming Superstars', 'Team Spirits'.

There should be a space for children to sign up in the middle of the poster, and pictures (from magazines, for example) all around the edges. The children could even bring in pictures from home of themselves engaged in the activities.

If you choose your tribes carefully, most children will belong to two, three or even four tribes—the more, the better.

Take some time during the week, after these assorted posters have been made, to point out that we are more interconnected than we might have realized. We are all in several tribes. If you are really clever, you can do a few Venn diagrams to show the interconnectedness of the tribes.

The point of this exercise is to show that children have a great deal in common with others whom they may not know very well. It will also show them that they have much in common with those children they had previously thought were in a wholly different group. Throughout the week, try to encourage the children to have a conversation with someone they do not know very well but who shares an interest with them. For example, if they like skateboarding, talk to someone else who enjoys it—but make sure that the person is someone they do not know very well. This should help everyone to see that:

- We are all connected to each other.
- We all belong to each other.
- We should all care for each other.
- We are all each other's neighbour.

KEEP IT IN MIND

Saying of the week

'If you judge people, you have no time to love them'

MOTHER TERESA OF CALCUTTA

GOD'S OWN GROUND FORCE

> God blesses those people who are treated badly for doing right. They belong to the kingdom of heaven.
>
> MATTHEW 5:10

─○ ◎ ● **GOD'S GUIDELINE** ● ◎ ○─

All of God's guidelines are relevant to this lesson and circle time.

Jesus says that all of God's guidelines can be hard to live by. But in today's Bible story, the parable of the farmer, Jesus said that he did not want us to be the sort of people who hear God's message about how we should live, and who make a good start, but then give up when it becomes obvious that we might face difficulties, hardship or opposition.

─○ ◎ ● ● ◎ ○─

THE PARABLE OF THE FARMER (1)

That same day Jesus left the house and went out beside Lake Galilee, where he sat down to teach. Such large crowds gathered around him that he had to sit in a boat, while the people stood on the shore. Then he taught them many things by using stories. He said:

A farmer went out to scatter seed in a field. While

the farmer was scattering the seed, some of it fell along the road and was eaten by birds. Other seeds fell on thin, rocky ground and quickly started growing because the soil wasn't very deep. But when the sun came up, the plants were scorched and dried up, because they did not have enough roots. Some other seeds grew where thorn bushes grew up and choked the plants. But a few seeds did fall on good ground where the plants produced a hundred or sixty or thirty times as much as was scattered. If you have ears, pay attention! …

Now listen to the meaning of the story about the farmer:

The seeds that fell along the road are the people who hear the message about the kingdom, but don't understand it. Then the evil one comes and snatches the message from their hearts. The seeds that fell on rocky ground are the people who gladly hear the message and accept it straight away. But they don't have deep roots, and they don't last very long. As soon as life gets hard or the message gets them in trouble, they give up.

The seeds that fell among the thorn bushes are also people who hear the message. But they start worrying about the needs of this life and are fooled by the desire to get rich. So the message gets choked out, and they never produce anything. The seeds that fell on good ground are the people who hear and understand the message. They produce as much as hundred or sixty or thirty times what was planted.

MATTHEW 13:1–9, 18–23

Jesus became very famous and great crowds of people would follow him wherever he went. They came to be healed and to see miracles. They also came to hear his wise teaching.

One day, Jesus and his disciples came to the shore of the Sea of Galilee. Thousands of people followed him there, and they all crowded around Jesus so that only the people who were very near could see Jesus. This was a big problem, but Jesus came up with a very good solution. He climbed into a boat and sailed a little distance away from the shore. This meant that the crowd could all sit or stand on the shore and see

Jesus in his boat. They could also hear him, as he was only a little way away.

But there is a big difference between listening to what someone says to you and really taking it in and acting upon what you hear. All teachers know this problem, and Jesus was a great teacher! He knew that, now he was in the boat, they would be able to see and hear him. But would the people listen to the message really carefully? Would it sink into their hearts and grow there? Would it change their lives? Jesus wanted people to think about this problem. So he told them a story or parable. A parable is a story about something important, using images and pictures from people's everyday lives.

A parable gives a memorable mental picture that illustrates the teacher's message. Jesus knew that, like sitting in the boat, a parable would help people to see and hear what he was teaching. This was the parable he told them.

There was once a farmer who wanted to grow wheat in his field. As he scattered the wheat seeds, some of them fell on to the hard, well-trodden footpath that went across the field. These seeds were soon spotted by birds who picked them up and ate them.

Some of the seeds fell on to a part of the field that was very stony and full of flints. These seeds started to grow, but the soil was thin and the plants could not put down good roots. When the sun came out, it scorched the plants and they soon withered and died. Some of the seeds fell into the weedy patch at the edge of the field. These seeds tried to grow but there was too much competition from the weeds and thistles, and those wheat plants were weak and useless—they never pro-duced any ears of wheat. But some of the seeds fell on to the good, well-dug earth. These seeds grew into strong wheat plants, each of which produced great ears of wheat.

Later that day, Jesus' disciples admitted that they hadn't understood the story, so Jesus explained what it meant. He said that God sends a message to all of his people—the message that Jesus came to deliver. This message was about how to live and behave so we can please God and be our best selves. The seeds are like the message. The seeds and the message are always good. Jesus can give everyone God's message, but he can't make people hear it and live by it.

Some people are hard-hearted, like the hard footpath. The message is given to them but they ignore it and it quickly disappears as if it had never been—it is snatched away by evil. The seeds of Jesus' message never even take root in these people's hearts. Other people are like the seeds on the stony ground. The message is given to them and they are really keen at first to listen and try to live in the right way. They look really promising at first, showing lots of signs of trying to be their best selves. But they don't do the hard work of clearing out the stones, that is, learning to persevere in the face of difficulties. They are shallow and superficial people; their roots are not deep. When the heat is on and it becomes difficult to live in the right way, they give up. All that early promise dies and disappears.

Others are like the seeds in the thorn bushes. They would really like to grow and produce good corn but it's too difficult for them. All sorts of other things get in the way. They are consumed with worries, or they are too taken up with making money or looking good or shopping or socializing with friends or going to parties. All of those things fill up their lives so much that they crowd out any chance of letting the mess-age from God grow in their lives. The seed sown by God never produces any fruit. They don't give it enough time or space.

The last group of people is the group who hear the message and make sure it grows and is fruitful in their lives. They clear the weeds—the concerns of everyday life. They get rid of the stones—their fail-ings and weaknesses. They make sure the earth is dug and well tended. They make time and space and a big effort to ensure that God's message can take root in their lives and grow and show fruit.

BEGIN WITH AN ATTITUDE OF GRATITUDE

Start by being thankful for all the good things that came out of last week's circle time. Use this time to refer to, and critically review, successes recorded on the noticeboard. Refer to particular children and any successes they may have had, and note any other good outcomes from last week's circle time.

BIBLE STORY SUMMARY

The farmer

Remind the children that the story showed that how we choose to live affects how well we can manage to be our best selves. Are we a bit hard-hearted and resistant to the message about being our best selves? Or are we like the stony ground—a bit shallow at times? Are we good starters but poor finishers? Maybe we want to be good people but we don't persevere. When things get difficult, do we give up?

Or are we like the weed patch—distracted by the busyness of the world? Some people are much too busy living their life to give time and thought to working out how to live as their best possible selves. They would rather put the material world above the spiritual world.

The seeds in the good ground are the people who do the hard work of making sure their lives are stone-free and weed-free and dug, ready to receive the message about how to live in the best way possible.

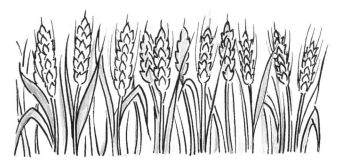

Today we will think about the stony ground. How can we learn to dig out the stones and be good at learning to persevere in the face of difficulties?

GET STARTED

Shoal of carp on the Central Line

Go around the circle putting the children into pairs. Ask the pairs to label themselves 'A' and 'B'.

This game is about excuses. For two minutes 'A' has to ask 'B' lots of questions about why certain things have not been done or completed. 'B' has to give an excuse each time. Sometimes, 'B' can give a completely mad excuse just to liven up the game! (The title of the game comes from a real incident when a furious director asked one of my fellow students at drama school why he was late for a rehearsal. With a charming smile the friend replied, 'So sorry. Train delayed—shoal of carp on the Central Line.') After two minutes, swap over so that 'B' asks 'A' questions.

If the class is struggling to invent questions, put a long list on the board or a flipchart. For example:

- Where is your reading book?
- Why didn't you tidy your room last night?
- Where is your PE kit?
- Did you go to your swimming lesson this week?
- Why did you argue back with your mum?
- Why haven't you done your maths homework?
- Why didn't you learn your spellings for the test this week?
- Why didn't you come to see me at break as I asked you to?
- Why didn't you set the table as you were asked to do?
- Why didn't you practise your piano/recorder/underwater basket-weaving (as appropriate)?
- Why didn't you go and see your grandma as you promised?
- Why didn't you water the plants in the classroom when you said you would?

GET REAL

Have a brief discussion about how blaming others for our failings or when things go wrong, excusing ourselves, breaking promises, and giving up too easily are all 'stones' that can stop us from being the kind of person who sticks at doing the right thing even when it's difficult. We have to learn to persevere in the face of difficulty if we want to be our best self.

Ask the children to think, in silence, for 30 seconds about something they found difficult but did not give up on. Go around the circle with the sentence, 'Although it was difficult, I stuck at…'

Examples of the above might be:

- Keeping a new year resolution.
- Going to chess club.
- Learning to skateboard, roller-skate, ride a bike, swim or sail.
- Doing a paper round in the winter.
- Playing the piano, learning all the times tables, learning to read.
- Walking the dog or caring for a pet as promised.
- Making time for homework instead of TV.
- Keeping a room tidy (be prepared for a good bit of self-deception at this stage!)

GET RIGHT

What would Jesus want us to do? Which of God's guidelines is relevant to this circle?

> **All of God's guidelines are relevant!**

Jesus says that all of God's guidelines can be hard to live by. But in the Bible story, the parable of the farmer, he said that he did not want us to be the sort of people who hear God's message about how we should live, and who make a good start, but then give up when it becomes obvious that we might face difficulties, hardship or opposition. If we can learn to stick at doing things we find difficult in one area of our lives, it means that if we really try hard, we can learn to stick at anything.

GET TOGETHER

In 'Get real', each member of the class mentioned something they found difficult but stuck at. Ask the class how they managed to persist, even though it was difficult. There is no need to go around again; just ask for hands up. This will weed out the well-meaning fibbers!

- What were some of the difficulties?
- What helped them?
- Who helped them?
- How did that person help?
- Who encouraged them?
- How did that person encourage them?
- What did they say to themselves to keep themselves going?

Make a note of these ideas. You will need to put them up on the noticeboard.

Explain to the class that you have chosen two or three of God's guidelines that you want them to try to stick to this week. Tell the children that they are to use their ideas for overcoming difficulties to help them. Explain that they will use the noticeboard to record their successes, and you will display the ideas they had for helping people to persevere in the face of difficulties.

KEEP GOING

This week's noticeboard

This week we looked at the parable of the farmer. We do not want to be 'stony ground'. We want our best selves to flourish.

Cover the noticeboard with brown sugar paper. Choose two or three of God's guidelines, which you particularly want the children to practise. Write them out under the words, 'This week we are trying to…', and put them up on the noticeboard.

Using the template on page 64, photocopy and colour some 'stones' and pin them randomly all over the noticeboard. Use two pins, one at the top and one at the bottom of each stone.

Around the edges or at the bottom of the noticeboard, rewrite and display the children's thoughts about how they were helped to persevere in the face of difficulties and opposition.

On a table beneath the noticeboard, or on a tin tray pinned to the bottom of the noticeboard, put a pile of wheat-shaped 'sheaves' (see template on page 65) and coloured pens. Tell the children that they can use the 'sheaves' paper and pens in the tray to record times when they have kept one of God's guidelines, even when it was difficult. Ask them to write about why it was difficult but how they managed to succeed. Tell them to mention anyone who helped them and how they were helped.

The children can remove the top pin from one of the stones, fold the stone down, and then pin their 'sheaf' to the noticeboard above the stone. The aim is to make it look as if they have dug up a stone and planted a success!

KEEP IT IN MIND

Saying of the week

Trying times are not the times to stop trying.

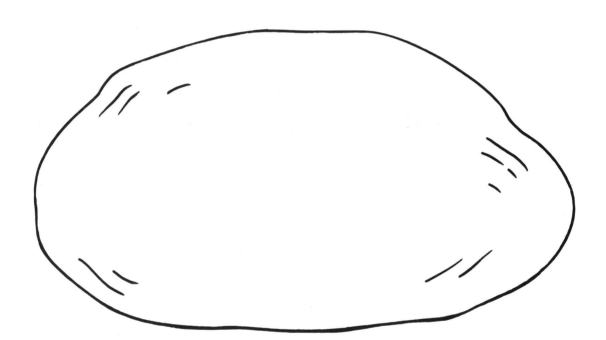

Reproduced with permission from *Stay Cool in School* published by BRF 2003 (1 84101 323 4)

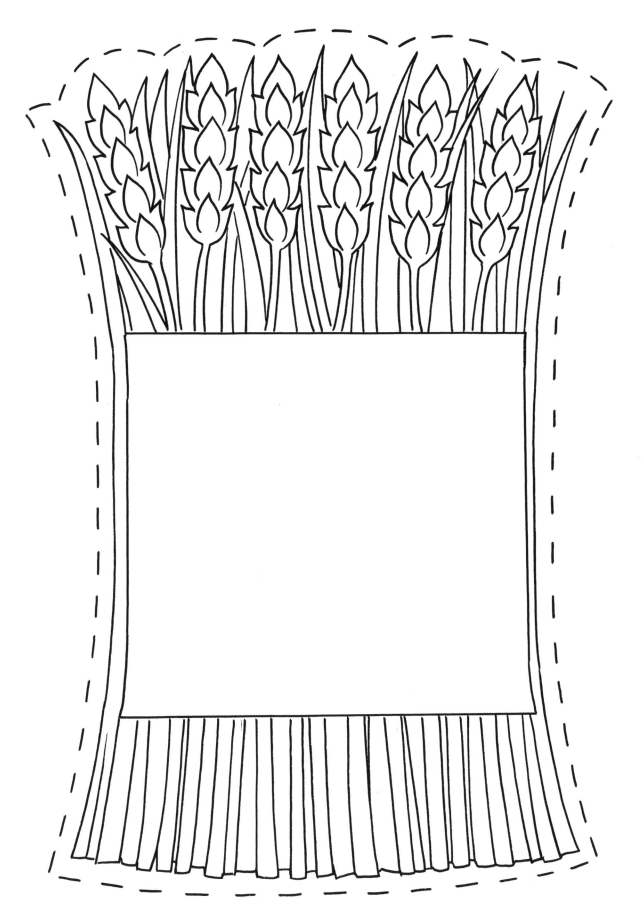

Reproduced with permission from *Stay Cool in School* published by BRF 2003 (1 84101 323 4)

How to see the wood from the trees

God blesses those people who depend only on him. They belong to the kingdom of heaven.

MATTHEW 5:3

○ ○ ● **GOD'S GUIDELINE** ● ○ ○

All of God's guidelines are relevant to this lesson and circle time.

Jesus says that all of God's guidelines can be hard to live by. But in the Bible story, the parable of the farmer, Jesus said that he did not want us to be the sort of people who hear God's message about how we should live, and who make a good start, but then give up when it becomes obvious that we might face difficulties, hardship or opposition.

THE PARABLE OF THE FARMER (2)

That same day Jesus left the house and went out beside Lake Galilee, where he sat down to teach. Such large crowds gathered around him that he had to sit in a boat, while the people stood on the shore. Then he taught them many things by using stories. He said:

A farmer went out to scatter seed in a field. While the farmer was scattering the seed, some of it fell along the road and was eaten by birds. Other seeds fell on thin, rocky ground and quickly started growing because the soil wasn't very deep. But when the sun came up, the plants were scorched and dried up, because they did not have enough roots. Some other seeds grew where thorn bushes grew up and choked the plants. But a few seeds did fall on good ground where the plants produced a hundred or sixty or thirty times as much as was scattered. If you have ears, pay attention! …

Now listen to the meaning of the story about the farmer:

The seeds that fell along the road are the people who hear the message about the kingdom, but don't understand it. Then the evil one comes and snatches the message from their hearts. The seeds that fell on rocky ground are the people who gladly hear the message and accept it straight away. But they don't have deep roots, and they don't last very long. As soon as life gets hard or the message gets them in trouble, they give up.

The seeds that fell among the thorn bushes are also people who hear the message. But they start worrying about the needs of this life and are fooled by the desire to get rich. So the message gets choked out, and they never produce anything. The seeds that fell on good ground are the people who hear and understand the message. They produce as much as a hundred or sixty or thirty times what was planted.

MATTHEW 13:1–9, 18–23

Jesus became very famous and great crowds of people would follow him wherever he went. They came to be healed and to see miracles. They also came to hear his wise teaching.

One day, Jesus and his disciples came to the shore of the Sea of Galilee. Thousands of people followed him there, and they all crowded around Jesus so that only the people who were very near could see Jesus. This was a big problem, but Jesus came up with a very good solution. He climbed into a boat and sailed a little distance away from the shore. This meant that the crowd could all sit or stand on the shore and see

Jesus in his boat. They could also hear him, as he was only a little way away.

But there is a big difference between listening to what someone says to you and really taking it in and acting upon what you hear. All teachers know this problem, and Jesus was a great teacher! He knew that, now he was in the boat, they would be able to see and hear him. But would the people listen to the message really carefully? Would it sink into their hearts and grow there? Would it change their lives? Jesus wanted people to think about this problem. So he told them a story or parable. A parable is a story about something important, using images and pictures from people's everyday lives.

A parable gives a memorable mental picture that illustrates the teacher's message. Jesus knew that, like sitting in the boat, a parable would help people to see and hear what he was teaching. This was the parable he told them.

There was once a farmer who wanted to grow wheat in his field. As he scattered the wheat seeds, some of them fell on to the hard, well-trodden footpath that went across the field. These seeds were soon spotted by birds who picked them up and ate them.

Some of the seeds fell on to a part of the field that was very stony and full of flints. These seeds started to grow, but the soil was thin and the plants could not put down good roots. When the sun came out, it scorched the plants and they soon withered and died. Some of the seeds fell into the weedy patch at the edge of the field. These seeds tried to grow but there was too much competition from the weeds and thistles, and those wheat plants were weak and useless—they never produced any ears of wheat. But some of the seeds fell on to the good, well-dug earth. These seeds grew into strong wheat plants, each of which produced great ears of wheat.

Later that day, Jesus' disciples admitted that they hadn't understood the story, so Jesus explained what it meant. He said that God sends a message to all of his people—the message that Jesus came to deliver. This message was about how to live and behave so we can please God and be our best selves. The seeds are like the message. The seeds and the message are always good. Jesus can give everyone God's message, but he can't make people hear it and live by it.

Some people are hard-hearted, like the hard foot-path. The message is given to them but they ignore it and it quickly disappears as if it had never been—it is snatched away by evil. The seeds of Jesus' message never even take root in these people's hearts. Other people are like the seeds on the stony ground. The message is given to them and they are really keen at first to listen and try to live in the right way. They look really promising at first, showing lots of signs of trying to be their best selves. But they don't do the hard work of clearing out the stones, that is, learning to persevere in the face of difficulties. They are shallow and superficial people; their roots are not deep. When the heat is on and it becomes difficult to live in the right way, they give up. All that early promise dies and disappears.

Others are like the seeds in the thorn bushes. They would really like to grow and produce good corn but it's too difficult for them. All sorts of other things get in the way. They are consumed with worries, or they are too taken up with making money or looking good or shopping or socializing with friends or going to parties. All of those things fill up their lives so much that they crowd out any chance of letting the message from God grow in their lives. The seed sown by God never produces any fruit. They don't give it enough time or space.

The last group of people is the group who hear the message and make sure it grows and is fruitful in their lives. They clear the weeds—the concerns of every-day life. They get rid of the stones—their failings and weaknesses. They make sure the earth is dug and well tended. They make time and space and a big effort to ensure that God's message can take root in their lives and grow and show fruit.

BEGIN WITH AN ATTITUDE OF GRATITUDE

Start by being thankful for all the good things that came out of last week's circle time. Use this time to refer to, and critically review, successes recorded on the noticeboard. Refer to particular children and any successes they may have had, and note any other good outcomes from last week's circle time.

BIBLE STORY SUMMARY

The farmer

Remind the children that the story showed that how we choose to live affects how well we can manage to be our best selves. Are we a bit hard-hearted and resistant to the message about being our best selves? Or are we like the stony ground—a bit shallow at times? Are we good starters but poor finishers? Maybe we want to be good people but we don't persevere. When things get difficult, do we give up?

Or are we like the weed patch—distracted by the busyness of the world? Some people are much too busy living their life to give time and thought to working out how to live as their best possible selves. They would rather put the material world above the spiritual world.

The seeds in the good ground are the people who do the hard work of making sure their lives are stone-free and weed-free and dug, ready to receive the message about how to live in the best way possible.

Today we will think about the weed-filled ground. How can we manage to 'put first things first'?

Often we do not give much time to thinking about how we should live because we are too busy thinking about what we want to do from day to day. When we live like this, the concerns of the world around us occupy all of our thoughts, squeezing out the time we should use to think about how well we are living according to our set of moral values.

GET STARTED

Have a brief chat about how we sometimes get so caught up in busyness that we forget to think about big things such as 'What sort of person do I want to be?' or 'What do I think is important?' or 'How should I live my life?' Examples of busyness might be:

- Watching TV
- Being with friends
- Playing football
- Listening to music
- Playing PlayStation
- Skateboarding
- Chatting on the phone
- Playing with the dog
- Texting
- Going shopping
- Looking out of the window
- Going to the park
- Reading books
- Looking at magazines

This list is duplicated below. Photocopy the list before the lesson, and give a copy to each child. Explain to the class that there is nothing wrong with the activities listed. This is not going to be a 'Teacher says you should be spending more time preparing for SATS and less time listening to Westlife' sort of lesson!

Ask the children to number their top two activities according to how much time they spend doing them. For example, if they spend most time on their skateboard, that gets a '1'. If TV is next, that gets a '2'. Allow about two minutes for this.

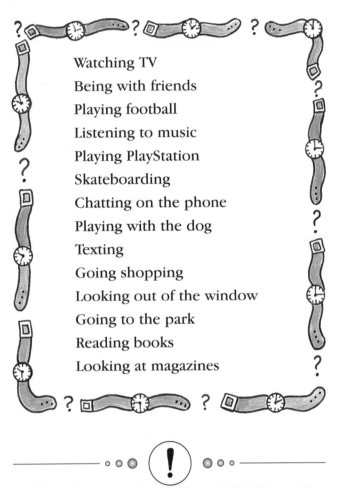

Watching TV

Being with friends

Playing football

Listening to music

Playing PlayStation

Skateboarding

Chatting on the phone

Playing with the dog

Texting

Going shopping

Looking out of the window

Going to the park

Reading books

Looking at magazines

GET REAL

Put the children into groups of four. To do this, either go round the circle counting them into fours or let them move about the circle, get into groups of four and then sit back in the circle. It does not matter if best friends sit together for this circle time.

Ask the groups to go around with the sentence 'The two activities that I spend most time on are…'

GET RIGHT

Bring the class back into the circle. Explain that the activities on the list are examples of things that can occupy much of our time and thinking. In the parable of the farmer, Jesus said that some people hear about trying to live as their best selves but the concerns and busyness of the world around drive all thoughts of it from their minds. But really we should try to keep living as our best selves all the time. As we go about our everyday lives, doing the things we enjoy, we should not let the thought, 'Am I being my best self?' ever leave our minds.

Which of God's guidelines is relevant to this circle?

> All of them—just as in the circle time about the stony ground. We need to think about how we can be our best selves while engaged in our favourite activities.

GET TOGETHER

Have a class discussion about how difficult it is to keep thinking about our behaviour and being self-critical.

Ask the groups to think about ways they can be their best selves while doing the things they enjoy. Ask them to write down their ideas next to the top two activities on their lists. For example, if they spend a lot of time texting each other, they could write, 'Never text gossip.' If they do a lot of skateboarding, they could write, 'Don't laugh at those who are a bit hopeless. Encourage them instead.' If they most enjoy TV, they could write, 'Try not to always argue when someone else wants to watch a different programme. Try to suggest taking turns.' If they often go to the park, they could write, 'Don't hang about in the little kids' area.'

These are only ideas. Your class will know how they can be thoughtful in their behaviour. Ensure that they work in their groups. This will help them to come up with more ideas than if they struggle alone. When they have thought of two each, go around the circle and ask each child to tell the circle one of their suggestions.

can write out ways in which they have tried to be their best selves. They can then stick these 'weed-free' patches on the green noticeboard. Aim to cover as much of the board as possible by the end of the week. Label the noticeboard: 'We are trying to keep our lives weed-free and able to flower.'

KEEP GOING

This week's noticeboard

Cover the board with backing paper and let the children scribble weeds all over it in different shades of green. Make sure it doesn't look at all neat or tidy. Then make several photocopies of the picture overleaf of a flower in a patch of clear earth. Ask the children to colour them in however they choose, as long as they make the earth pale brown.

Throughout the week, the children can take a flower and colour it in. On the pale brown earth they

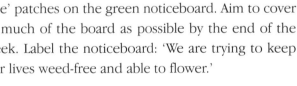

KEEP IT IN MIND

Saying of the week

It's not what you do, it's the way that you do it!

Reproduced with permission from *Stay Cool in School* published by BRF 2003 (1 84101 323 4)

BECAUSE HE'S WORTH IT

When you do good deeds, don't try to show off. If you do, you won't get a reward from your Father in heaven… When you give to the poor, don't let anyone know about it. Then your gift will be given in secret. Your Father knows what is done in secret, and he will reward you.

MATTHEW 6:1, 3–4

GOD'S GUIDELINE

Don't show off, letting everyone know how good or clever or generous you are. Instead, go about your life quietly and with humility, trying to do your best.

THE PARABLE OF THE PHARISEE AND THE TAX COLLECTOR

Jesus told a story to some people who thought they were better than others and who looked down on everyone else.

Two men went into the temple to pray. One was a Pharisee and the other a tax collector. The Pharisee stood over by himself and prayed, 'God, I thank you that I am not greedy, dishonest, and unfaithful in marriage like other people. And I am really glad that I am not like that tax collector over there. I go without eating for two days a week, and I give you one tenth of all I earn.'

The tax collector stood off at a distance and did not think he was good enough even to look up towards heaven. He was so sorry for what he had done that he pounded his chest and prayed, 'God have pity on me! I am such a sinner.'

Then Jesus said, 'When the two men went home, it was the tax collector and not the Pharisee who was pleasing to God. If you put yourself above others, you will be put down. But if you humble yourself, you will be honoured.'

LUKE 18:9–14

Has anyone ever made you feel stupid? Have you ever had to listen to someone tell you how great they are at swimming or dancing or football, so that in the end they've managed to make you feel a complete failure? Have you ever done the same thing to other people?

We can be very good at telling everyone about our successes, but we don't always notice that we do things wrong as well. For example, that person who is busy telling you how marvellous they are at football isn't noticing that their endless boasting is not very kind. Or what about the person who thinks they are very popular but all they really want is a big audience to brag to? Or perhaps there's someone who likes the feeling of having lots of friends around , but then they spend their time talking about people behind their back?

We have to be very careful that we don't get so impressed with ourselves that we fail to notice our faults. Jesus used to get quite cross with people who did this. He called them 'hypocrites'. They were people who thought they were great, but were not really trying to live good, humble lives at all.

One group of people, who Jesus knew were not living the right way, were called the Pharisees. Jesus knew that if you are to be your best self, you must have humility—you must be able to admit your faults. But the Pharisees believed they were perfect because they knew and kept all of the tiny details of the Jewish law, so they had come to believe that they were better than everyone else. They were not bad people, but they were proud, and this pride was not pleasing to Jesus.

So one day Jesus told this story to try to explain to the Pharisees that God prefers people who have humility and are honest about themselves and their faults—that is, people who go quietly about their lives trying to be their best selves.

There were two men praying in the temple. One was a Pharisee. He wanted everyone to know how rich, generous and pious he was. When he prayed, he stood in the middle of the temple and made sure everyone could see him. He also made sure everyone could hear him! He prayed in a big loud voice:

'Oh God, I thank you that I am not greedy or dishonest like everyone else. I thank you that I am nothing like that tax gatherer over there. I fast two days a week and give you a tenth of my money.'

He made sure everyone was impressed with his holiness and generosity. But there was another man praying in the temple that day as well. He was a tax collector. No one really liked him as he collected taxes from the Jewish people and gave the money to the occupying Roman army. He too wanted to pray, but when he prayed he hung his head in deep shame and prayed like this:

'Dear God, please help me. I know I am a sinner. Have pity on me.'

Jesus said, 'I am telling you, it was the tax collector and not the Pharisee who went home right with God. Anyone who thinks he is great will be humbled, but those who know they have real faults will be helped and made great by God.' Jesus believed that we should go about our life doing good things quietly and humbly. He said that God knows what we do, and God is the only person we need to impress.

BEGIN WITH AN ATTITUDE OF GRATITUDE

Start by being thankful for all the good things that came out of last week's circle time. Use this time to refer to, and critically review, successes recorded on the noticeboard. Refer to particular children and any successes they may have had, and note any other good outcomes from last week's circle time.

BIBLE STORY SUMMARY

The Pharisee and the tax collector

This week's story was about two men. One was a Pharisee. Pharisees were very well respected and highly regarded in the community. He thought that because he kept every last detail of the Jewish law, he was better than other people were. He was proud and thought he was earning God's pleasure by doing these things.

The other man was a tax collector. Tax collectors were not well respected. No one was keen to have a tax collector round for tea! But he was a humble man who was very honest with himself and with God. He knew he did bad things, as we all do! With true humility he asked God to forgive him. Jesus said that God will humble the proud and make the humble great.

In the Bible, Jesus says God will love you even if you do things wrong, as long as you are humble and honest about your faults, say sorry and ask for his help. He said that God prefers it if we go about our life doing good things quietly and humbly, without letting everyone know how marvellous we think we are being! He said that God knows what we do, and God is the only person we need to impress.

GET STARTED

This cross-the-circle game is designed to encourage children to be honest with themselves.

Cross the circle if you have ever:

- Looked at a pile of wet towels on the bathroom floor, thought, 'Someone else will pick them up' and left the room.
- Borrowed something without asking.
- Eaten the last biscuit in the tin.
- Borrowed something and not given it back.
- Made a face behind someone's back.
- Been a bit of a show-off.
- 'Forgotten' to give your mum or dad the change.
- Said you were ill when you wanted to get out of doing something.
- Been a bit too keen to tell everyone how good you are at PlayStation.
- Said you'd do something and then 'forgotten'—like walking the dog/cleaning out the rabbit/feeding the fish.
- Eaten biscuits or crisps in your bedroom and then stuffed the wrappers or bags under your bed.
- Kicked your brother or sister under the table.
- Told everyone how nice you had been to a new girl.
- Boasted about all the things you can do on your skateboard.
- Quietly left the kitchen when it was time to clear the table or do the washing-up.
- Deliberately got your brother or sister into trouble by telling on them.
- Let everyone one know how well you did in your ballet exam.
- Told your mum you had tidied your room when really all you had done was to pick up all the clothes from the floor and dump them in the dirty laundry basket.

Use as many or as few of these suggestions as you choose. The aim is to make sure everyone in the group moves at least once, so invent other age-

appropriate examples. Include light-hearted examples of common childhood dishonesty, idleness or pride as well as more serious things.

By the end, everyone should have moved. If not, finish with, 'Cross the circle if you have ever told a fib—even a very little one.'

Say to the class, 'Well done! It's great to know I have a really honest class. Nobody, but nobody, is perfect!'

GET REAL

Tell the class that you want them to think about some of the things that they know they could do better—for example, anything from the above list that caused them to cross the circle, or anything else that they know is a fault. Give them 20 seconds' silent thinking time.

Now give everyone a piece of paper and ask them to write down something they would like to work at improving. Give them the opening, 'If tomorrow was New Year's Day, my resolution would be to…' They must not put their name on this paper. Ask them to fold the paper up and stow it in a pocket.

(There is no spoken round in this circle, to avoid embarrassment.)

GET RIGHT

Which of God's guidelines is relevant to this circle?

> Don't show off, letting everyone know how good or clever or generous you are. Instead, go about your life quietly and with humility, trying to do your best.

This is exactly what Jesus thought the Pharisee should have done.

GET TOGETHER

Have a class discussion about the difficulties we all have in thinking about our faults, and why it is so pleasant to dwell instead on our successes. Is it easy to be self-centred?

We all have faults and difficulties and we are going to try to overcome them, but that is easier if we make life better for each other and not more difficult. Jesus said that we had to do good deeds in secret. The best good deed we can do this week is to help each other to be our best selves.

First ask the children to think of the things they do that might cause other people pain and lead them to behave badly. This will include anything they do that makes another person feel stupid, unloved, unliked or bossed around. All these things will lead other people into behaving badly. Here are some ideas to get people started. Things that don't help others to be their best selves are:

- Boasting, which makes others feel stupid
- Winding people up
- Calling people unkind names

- Laughing at people's failings
- Laughing at people's appearance
- Talking about people behind their backs

The children will be able to think of a huge list! Write down all the suggestions. Now ask them to think of things they can do which will help other people to feel happy and good about life. Anything you do for someone that makes them feel competent, capable, loved, liked and not pushed around, is going to help them to be their best selves.

Things that we can do to help each other be our best selves are:

- Smiling at people
- Listening attentively when people talk to you
- Laughing at people's jokes in a kind way
- Listening with sympathy if someone else has a problem
- Being generous with our friendship—not leaving people out of conversations or games
- Never talking behind someone's back

Again, the children's list of ideas will be huge. Record their suggestions on a separate piece of paper. Say how pleased you are that they know how to do good and make life better for each other, and that they know how to do this quietly and with humility. Explain that throughout the week they are going to be doing things from the 'helpful' list for each other. They are going to be kind to each other, and the difference will show— but they are going to do these things secretly. Then explain how this week's noticeboard is going to work.

Pin the angel in the middle of the noticeboard.

Explain to the children that when people do good, kind things for each other they are making the world a better place. The children know what these things are because you wrote down all their good ideas on the 'helpful' list. They know how to take care of each other. But we must do these things quietly, not looking for praise or recognition. We must do the right thing simply because it is the right thing to do!

Explain that some people believe we have guardian angels who take care of us—but we never know they are doing it. Tell the children that this week we are going to be each other's guardian angels. We are going to behave kindly towards each other, without telling anyone we are doing it.

We will know if it is working, because if you have had a happy day at school you can take a silver pen or crayon and colour in one segment of the angel's wing. The more children have happy days, the more the wings will turn to silver. But all the good will be done in secret!

Write across the top of the board: 'This week we are all being each other's guardian angel.'

Underneath the angel, write: 'Angels work in secret! Be an angel!'

Now ask the children to write out their ideas from the 'helpful' list on separate pieces of paper and decorate them. Pin the ideas around the edges of the noticeboard.

Throughout the week, encourage children to remember to colour in a segment of the angel's wings if they have had a happy day at school. Also, encourage the children to be their kindest selves towards each other, never forgetting that we are doing these kind things in secret.

KEEP GOING

This week's noticeboard

Photocopy the picture of the guardian angel overleaf. Enlarge it as big as your photocopier can manage. Before the circle time, ask a couple of children to colour in the clothes. *Leave the wings uncoloured.*

KEEP IT IN MIND

Saying of the week

When you are feeling down—look up!

Reproduced with permission from *Stay Cool in School* published by BRF 2003 (1 84101 323 4)

You can't take it with you

> Don't store up treasures on earth! Moths and rust can destroy them, and thieves can break in and steal them. Instead, store up your treasures in heaven, where moths and rust cannot destroy them, and thieves cannot break in and steal them. Your heart will always be where your treasure is.
>
> MATTHEW 6:19–21
>
> You cannot serve both God and money.
>
> MATTHEW 6:24

─ ∘ ◦ ◉   **GOD'S GUIDELINE**   ◉ ◦ ∘ ─

Don't put all your efforts into being rich—you can't take it with you! Instead, work really hard at being your best self.

─ ∘ ◦ ◉ 📖 ◉ ◦ ∘ ─

THE PARABLE OF THE RICH YOUNG MAN

A man came to Jesus and asked, 'Teacher, what good thing must I do to have eternal life?'

Jesus said to him, 'Why do you ask me about what is good? Only God is good. If you want to have eternal life, you must obey his commandments.'

'Which ones?' the man asked.

Jesus answered, 'Do not murder. Be faithful in marriage. Do not steal. Do not tell lies about others. Respect your father and mother. And love others as much as you love yourself.' The young man said, 'I have obeyed all these. What else must I do?'

Jesus replied, 'If you want to be perfect, go and sell everything you own! Give the money to the poor, and you will have riches in heaven. Then come and be my follower.' When the young man heard this, he was sad, because he was very rich.

Jesus said to his disciples, 'It's terribly hard for rich people to get into the kingdom of heaven! In fact, it's easier for a camel to go through the eye of a needle than for a rich person to get into God's kingdom.'

When the disciples heard this, they were greatly surprised and asked, 'How can anyone ever be saved?'

Jesus looked straight at them and said, 'There are some things that people cannot do, but God can do anything.'

Peter replied, 'Remember, we have left everything to be your followers! What will we get?'

Jesus answered:

Yes, all of you have become my followers. And so in the future world, when the Son of Man sits on his glorious throne, I promise that you will sit on twelve thrones to judge the twelve tribes of Israel. All who have given up home or brothers and sisters or father and mother or children or land for me will be given a hundred times as much. They will also have eternal life. But many who are now first will be last, and many who are last will be first.

MATTHEW 19:16–30

Jesus' disciples were not rich men. Before they met Jesus, they had all had different jobs. Some had been fishermen, others had had quite well-paid jobs, but now they were all very poor because they had given up everything to follow Jesus.

One day, Jesus and his disciples were talking together when suddenly the disciples saw someone very different from them come running down the road. This man was not a poor man, or even an ordinary man, and he was definitely not a fisherman! The disciples looked at him and were impressed. He was young, and obviously came from a very rich family. He was wearing all the latest and most fashionable clothes. These were clothes the disciples could not have afforded in a million years! He also had a very smart haircut and a posh accent. They could see straight away that he was a rich young man who could buy whatever he wanted.

The disciples quickly made way for the rich man. Going up to Jesus, he asked, 'Teacher, could you please tell me what good thing I must do, so that I can be sure I have eternal life?' Jesus looked at the young man steadily. 'You must keep the commandments,' said Jesus. The Ten Commandments are the rules that all good Jewish people live by. 'Oh,' said the young man confidently, 'I have always kept the commandments. What else do I need to do?' Again, Jesus looked at him, and then he said, 'Sell everything you own and give the money to the poor. Then you will have riches in heaven. After you have done that, come back here and you can follow me.'

The rich young man was devastated. Sell all his things? Give his money away? Be poor? No, he couldn't do that. That was too hard. Sadly, he turned and walked away. There was no way he could deliberately become poor.

Jesus watched the young man as he walked off down the road. 'You know,' he said, as the young man disappeared from view, 'it's easier for a camel to get through the eye of a needle than it is for a rich man to get into heaven.'

'What?' said the disciples. 'You must be joking! Everything is easier for rich people. If it's too hard for a rich young man like him, then who is going to be able to get into the kingdom of heaven?'

Jesus smiled at them. 'It's not up to you. It's up to God. You will be fine, though.'

Jesus had to explain to them that God's kingdom does not operate like this world. In this world, the rich young man had everything he wanted, and he thought he could do things to guarantee that he would have eternal life. But Jesus had to explain to all of them that in God's kingdom, God is in charge. It's entirely up to him who gets into heaven. One thing you can be sure of, however, is that you must not put anything before God. That was why Jesus told the man to sell everything. He had to show God that he wanted to get to heaven more than anything. And that was why the disciples would be fine, because they had put Jesus before everything else in their lives. Jesus said that we have to put wanting to be our best selves before everything else.

BEGIN WITH AN ATTITUDE OF GRATITUDE

Start by being thankful for all the good things that came out of last week's circle time. Use this time to refer to, and critically review, successes recorded on the noticeboard. Refer to particular children and any successes they may have had, and note any other good outcomes from last week's circle time.

BIBLE STORY SUMMARY

The rich young man

This week's story was about a rich young man who wanted to know how to get eternal life. However, when he learned that it would mean putting God before everything and giving up all that he owned, he could not do it and so went away sadly. Jesus told his followers that we cannot make ourselves acceptable to God by doing certain things. What we have to do is to put God first in our lives and then the rest is up to God.

GET STARTED

Time-limited Zoom and Eek

The only way to win this game is to put others before yourself. The object of the game is to go right around the circle with every child having said the word 'zoom' within a given time limit, usually one minute. (Have a timer visible.) To make it difficult, each child is also allowed to say 'eek' just once. If they say 'eek', they reverse the direction of the zoom.

The difficulty is this: it is good fun to take control of the game and say 'eek', but if you do so near the end of the game, it may not be possible to get the 'zoom' back to the original starting point within the minute! Children therefore have to balance their desire to say 'eek', take control of the game and reverse the direction of the 'zoom', with their desire to have a group success and get the 'zoom' back to the original starting point within the minute. The group's desire to 'win' may pressurize them into forgoing their desire to say 'eek'.

Cross-the-circle

Cross the circle if:

- You are currently saving up for something.
- You dislike anyone touching your possessions.
- You spend lots of time planning what you are going to buy.
- You sometimes feel jealous of other people's possessions.
- You sometimes find it difficult to share your possessions.

GET REAL

Go around the circle. Each child begins the sentence with, 'The thing I would find it hardest to give away is my…'

GET RIGHT

What would Jesus want us to do? In the story, Jesus told the young man that he would never get anywhere with God until he learned to put God first. What do God's guidelines ask us to do?

> Don't put all your efforts into being rich—you can't take it with you! Instead, work really hard at being your best self.

GET TOGETHER

Have a discussion about whether or not we think we might be materialistic, like the rich young man in the story. Do things that are ours become too important to us in our lives? Do we need to try to find ways to become less worried about possessions and more concerned about what sort of person we are? How difficult is that in the materialistic 21st century?

How can we work hard to be our best selves and not just to be rich? Explain to the children that Jesus told the young man to sell everything and give the money to the poor. He said this because he knew that, for this young man, money was the most important thing in his life.

What is the most important thing in our lives? It should be being our best self. Maybe, though, it is our possessions, our money, our friends or our comfortable lives. How can we learn to put these things aside? If the class have plenty of good ideas for how they might do this, that's good. Write them down and implement them. If they are struggling, you could try the following.

Perhaps the children might think about 'giving up' something that they enjoy but perhaps isn't really

good for them, for half an hour during the following week. This should be an activity, not food. In place of the activity they are giving up, they could do something that would help them to work at being their best self. The rich young man obviously put too much store by his money. What might we try to manage without? Activities we might give up for a half an hour or an hour this week might be:

- Playing on the PlayStation
- Talking on the phone to someone you only saw an hour ago
- Watching TV
- Reading magazines
- Spending hours in front of a mirror
- Shopping

Ask the children for their own suggestions.

Activities we could take up in their place might be:

- Talking with a parent
- Laying a table so that people can eat and talk together
- Reading a book
- Tidying a room
- Writing to a relation
- Phoning a grandparent, just for a brief chat

Again, the children will have good suggestions. It is important to explain that thinking about our priorities in life is difficult. We have to go on, through our whole lives, thinking about whether we are putting the right things first.

KEEP GOING

This week's noticeboard

Make a large collage picture from magazines, catalogues and so on, of all of the things the children use to fill their time (and empty their purses!). Put the picture in the middle of the noticeboard. These are the things we put first in our lives and the things that are of great importance to us—for example, bikes, skateboards, clothes, TV, magazines, sweets, rollerblades, makeup, CDs, hair gel, PlayStation, lego, videos, the latest craze toy, collections of things and so on.

NB: Reiterate that there is nothing wrong with these things, but sometimes they get to be the most important things in our lives—more important than trying to be our best selves.

Around the outside of the noticeboard, surrounding the collage, ask the children to pin up a certificate, or a scroll or some other 'official' or signed document that you have designed, which details what they did in place of their usual activity. You could copy the one on this page.

For example, the certificate might read, 'Instead of... spending half an hour watching TV, I... helped my mum (or 'read a book', 'tidied my room', 'sorted out the rubbish under my bed', 'called a friend who had been a bit forgotten lately').

The class will come up with better suggestions. At the beginning of next week's circle time, you could talk about how they got on—if they managed it at all and, if they did, whether they found it difficult or strange.

KEEP IT IN MIND

Saying of the week

Your heart will always be where your treasure is.

Instead of... _____

_____

_____

_____

_____

_____

I... _____

_____

_____

_____

_____

signed... _____

Reproduced with permission from *Stay Cool in School* published by BRF 2003 (1 84101 323 4)

NO GIFT LIKE THE PRESENT

You are like light for the whole world. A city built on top of a hill cannot be hidden, and no one would light a lamp and put it under a clay pot. A lamp is placed on a lampstand, where it can give light to everyone in the house. Make your light shine, so that others will see the good that you do and will praise your Father in heaven.

MATTHEW 5:14–16

○ ○ ○ GOD'S GUIDELINE ○ ○ ○

All of God's guidelines are relevant to this lesson and circle time. We have to be watchful that we are our best selves at all times.

THE PARABLE OF THE FIVE SENSIBLE GIRLS AND FIVE SILLY GIRLS

Jesus said:

The kingdom of heaven is like what happened one night when ten girls took their oil lamps and went to a wedding to meet the groom. Five of the girls were foolish and five were wise. The foolish ones took their lamps, but no extra oil. The ones who were wise took along extra oil for their lamps.

The groom was late arriving, and the girls become drowsy and fell asleep. Then in the middle of the night someone shouted, 'Here's the groom! Come to meet him!'

When the girls got up and started getting their lamps ready, the foolish ones said to the others, 'Let us have some of your oil! Our lamps are going out.'

The girls who were wise answered, 'There's not enough oil for all of us! Go and buy some for yourselves.'

While the foolish girls were on their way to get some oil, the groom arrived. The girls who were ready went into the wedding, and the doors were closed. Later the other girls returned and shouted, 'Sir, sir! Open the door for us!'

But the groom replied, 'I don't even know you!'

So, my disciples, always be ready! You don't know the day or the time when all this will happen.

MATTHEW 25:1–13

Have you ever been told that you have to take something special in to school—for PE, for example—and then not really bothered to organize yourself properly and forgotten all about it? Maybe you've thought, 'Blow it, I'll sort all that out later!' But 'later' has a way of coming round sooner than you think! Suddenly PE day has arrived and you have gone off to school with nothing. You panic! You rush about trying to borrow bits from your friends, but it's no good. The teacher realizes you don't have any kit and you are in big trouble—so much trouble, in fact, that you have to sit out and watch everyone else run about the field in the summer sun, having a great time.

As you gloomily watch your friends high-jumping, triple-jumping, relay-racing and sprinting, you wish you had been better organized. But it's too late; you can't take part. If you had only listened carefully, remembered the teacher's instructions and spent time getting ready for the lesson it would have been you flying over the high-jump bar. Instead, you are sitting out and feeling really fed up.

One day Jesus told a story that was a bit like the story of the forgotten PE kit. It was the story of five silly girls who didn't get properly organized and missed out on the best party of their lives.

Jesus was explaining to a crowd of people that, although they thought they had all the time in the world to put their lives straight and start behaving as God wanted them to behave, they probably had less time than they thought. They should get organized now! Jesus said that no one knows when they will be called upon to account for themselves before God. What's more, if God comes and we cannot give a good account of ourselves, then we will not go to heaven to be with him. That is why we have to be ever ready.

As he was speaking, perhaps Jesus could see a group of young girls sitting nearby, only half listening to what he was saying. They were only half listening because they were also giggling with each other, fiddling with each other's hair and gossiping. Jesus looked at these girls and smiled. Now, how was he going to get them to listen? He knew he must get everyone to listen. He loved all people and did not want anyone to fail to get to be with God just because they had not known they had to be ready. So he told this story.

Once there were ten girls who were waiting to be collected to go to a big wedding party. The bridegroom himself was going to collect them. But they had a big problem. They were not quite sure what time they were to be collected. It was an evening party and it was dark outside so they had to keep popping out to see if the bridegroom was arriving.

Five of the girls had good oil lamps. (Oil lamps were the torches of Jesus' day.) They also had spare lamp oil. They could see along the road and were

keeping a careful watch. They were absolutely ready. As soon as the bridegroom arrived, they could leave. But the other five girls were hopeless! They left their lamps burning, they hadn't checked the oil levels and they had none spare.

The bridegroom was later than everyone ex-pected, and they all nodded off. Suddenly, there was a big commotion—someone brought a mess-age to say the bridegroom was on his way. The five sensible girls woke up, refilled their lamps from their spare oil supply and were up and off down the lane, looking out for the bridegroom by the light of their bright lamps.

But the silly girls woke up and had no lights. 'Lend us your oil,' they said to the sensible girls. 'No,' said the sensible girls. 'If we take oil from our lamps then no one will be able to see their way. Go to the shop quickly and get some more oil. Why did you not plan ahead?' And they sped off down the lane.

The silly girls were just not ready. While they were at the shop, the bridegroom arrived, collected the sensible girls and took them off to the wedding party. Eventually the silly girls found their way to the party, but it was too late. They asked the men on the door to let them in but they just said, 'We don't know who you are. All of the guests came with the bridegroom. We can't let you in.'

The silly girls were so sad and cross with them-selves. If only they had been sensible, been prepared and vigilant. But it was too late now. They were shut out of the party.

Jesus looked at the crowd, and especially at the girls—who were now paying full attention. 'The kingdom of heaven is like that,' he said. 'Be ready. You do not know when you will be called to account for your life. God will call for you and you must be ready.'

So, like the girls with the lamps and the child with the PE kit, we must remember to be ready and get on with sorting out our lives now. It is no good saying, 'I will get round to being my best self and living as God wants me to live "one day."' That may be too late. Jesus said that all people must be their best selves all the time.

BEGIN WITH AN ATTITUDE OF GRATITUDE

Start by being thankful for all the good things that came out of last week's circle time. Use this time to refer to, and critically review, successes recorded on the noticeboard. Refer to particular children and any successes they may have had, and note any other good outcomes from last week's circle time.

BIBLE STORY SUMMARY

The five sensible girls and five silly girls

Jesus told the people that they must be ready to face God at any time. No one knows the day or the hour when he will come and call upon us to give an account of our lives. Jesus illustrated this with the story of ten girls who were going to a wedding party. Five of the girls were sensible. They were ready with oil in their lamps. As soon as the bridegroom called for them, they were ready and set off with him to the party. The five silly girls were not ready. They were asleep when the bridegroom called for them, their lamps were out, they had run out of oil and they missed the party. Jesus said that we must be like the sensible girls, always ready to face God, or we might miss the chance to be with him.

GET STARTED

Fruit salad *or* Rainbow

Play a quick muddling up game, such as 'Fruit salad' or 'Rainbow'. For 'Fruit salad', go around the circle giving each child the name of a fruit. For 'Rainbow', go around the circle giving each child a colour of the rainbow.

When each child has been given a fruit or a colour,

call out one fruit/colour and ask all those children to move to another part of the room. Carry on until the children are standing around in random groups.

When they are all muddled up, divide the children into groups of four. Give each group four small pieces of paper (A5) and a pencil. Ask each child to write something that they are pleased they have done during their time in the school. If they can't think of anything, the group can help them by reminding them of the good things they have done. For example, 'You were great in the school play', or, 'You were really kind to me when I was new', or, 'You always make me laugh when I feel fed up.'

Give them four or five minutes for this at most, and bring the group back into the circle.

GET REAL

Remind the children that doing the right thing is like putting oil in your lamp. Each of the good things they have done has helped the flame of their best selves to shine more brightly. Go around the circle with the sentence, 'I am pleased that I...' The children can read out what is on their piece of paper.

GET RIGHT

What would Jesus want us to do? In the Bible story, he said that we were to try to be our best selves at all times. So which of God's guidelines is relevant to this circle?

> All of them! If we have to be watchful that we are our best selves at all times, we can't afford to forget about any of the guidelines.

GET TOGETHER

Have a discussion about the sort of things that distract us from concentrating on being our best selves. If we thought the world was going to end tomorrow, would we do things differently, and behave towards others differently, today?

Photocopy the 'drops of oil' printed opposite and cut them out. Put them in a bag and pull them out one at a time.

Encourage the class to discuss how they could earn each 'drop' during the coming week. For example, when you pull out, 'Don't show off, letting everyone know how good or clever or generous you are', they might suggest something like, 'Next time there is a test, we could be given back the results and keep them to ourselves, and not tell everyone if we have done well.'

Record the class suggestions.

KEEP GOING

This week's noticeboard

It helps us to understand the story of the sensible and silly girls if we think of it like this:

- The flame is our best selves.
- Each drop of oil is a good action.
- This oil acts as fuel for keeping our best selves alight.

Photocopy the drawing of a first-century oil lamp on page 90. Colour it either terracotta or pale beige. Pin it at the bottom of the noticeboard. Across the very top of the board write, *either* 'We are trying to keep the flame of our best selves burning' *or* 'We are trying to keep our lamps ready like the five sensible girls.'

Make eight or nine more photocopies of the 'drops' opposite, and cut them out. If you want to

make it more interesting, copy them on to yellow paper so that they look more like drops of oil.

Pin a deep tinfoil tray to the base of the noticeboard. Put all of the drops into the tray. Tie a pen to a piece of string about two feet long and attach it to the noticeboard by the tray. Next, find a large, clear plastic fizzy drink bottle. Cut the spout and neck off the bottle so that it has straight sides. Label it 'Our spare oil'.

Lastly, using either red, yellow and orange coloured card or white card that you have coloured, cut out about fifty strips of card, about 10cm long x 1cm wide. These are beams of light which will shine out from the lamp. Put them in a bag firmly pinned to the bottom of the noticeboard or put them in a box.

Ask the children to notice whenever they do something that means they have kept one of God's guidelines. Tell them to take a drop of oil from the tray, write what they did on the back of the drop, and put it in the 'spare oil' bottle. Then they can take a beam of light and pin it above the lamp as if it were radiating from the wick.

Try to fill up the whole board with light, and the bottle with oil, by the end of the week.

KEEP IT IN MIND

Saying of the week

> This little light of mine, I'm gonna let it shine!

Be aware of your own faults but never judge or criticize other people.

Treat other people as you would have them treat you.

Look into your heart and be honest, especially with yourself.

Don't put all your efforts into being rich—you can't take it with you! Instead, work really hard at being your best self.

Stay calm, do not be angry with each other, never take revenge and never try to get your own back or get even.

Be loving and forgiving to all people, even to those you really don't like and who don't like you.

Don't show off, letting everyone know how good or clever or generous you are. Instead, go about your life quietly and with humility, trying to do your best.

Don't worry too much about what you will wear or what you will eat. The most important thing is to live as God wants you to live, to ask for his help and trust in his care.

Reproduced with permission from *Stay Cool in School* published by BRF 2003 (1 84101 323 4)

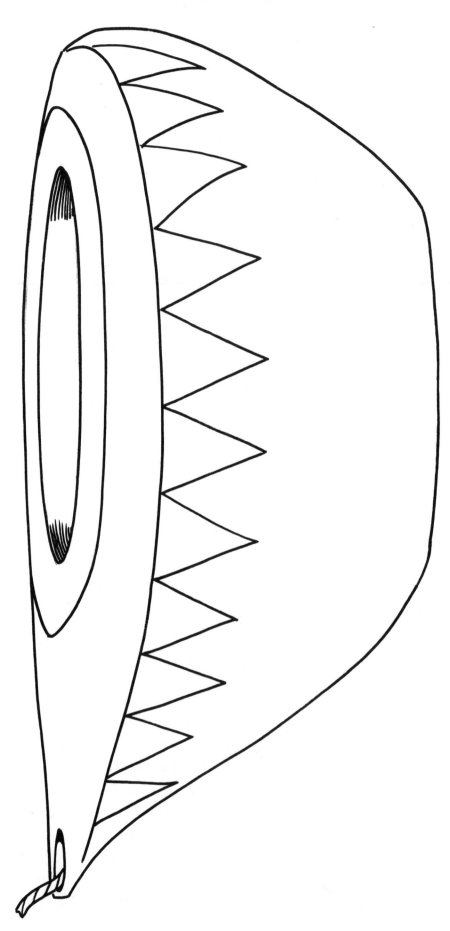

Reproduced with permission from *Stay Cool in School* published by BRF 2003 (1 84101 323 4)

READY, STEADY, COOK UP A GREAT LIFE

You are like salt for everyone on earth. But if salt no longer tastes like salt, how can it make food salty? All it is good for is to be thrown out and walked on.

MATTHEW 5:13

GOD'S GUIDELINE

All of God's guidelines are relevant to this lesson and circle time. If we live by the guidelines, we help to make the school into the best place it can be.

THE PARABLE OF THE YEAST IN THE DOUGH

Jesus also said, 'The kingdom of heaven is like what happens when a woman mixes a little yeast into three big batches of flour. Finally, all the dough rises.'

MATTHEW 13:33

It was morning, before the day grew too hot. Jesus was teaching hundreds of people who had come to hear him speak. He was teaching them about the kingdom of heaven—that is, God's kingdom. He was in a boat and the people were by the side of the lake. There were men and women and children, and they were all hungry to hear Jesus' words of wisdom.

Some of the women who were there started to worry that their families would get hungry for some food pretty soon as well! Usually the women would have been at home, busy with their housework. Some would have been drawing water from the wells and some would have been sifting the flour and kneading the dough, ready to make the bread for the day. But today they were all at the lakeside.

Suddenly one woman stood up. 'I must go,' she whispered to her friend. 'I must get home and do the baking or there will be no bread for the family tonight. Anyway, I don't really understand this too well—I can't see how it applies to me. So there's no point in staying.'

She looked across at Jesus. He was telling a group of farmers that the kingdom of heaven is not something visible and showy, like the kingdoms of the world's mighty rulers. The kingdom of heaven is tiny, like a little mustard seed. But, just as a mustard seed grows to become a huge tree, so, if the kingdom of heaven is planted in your heart, even as a little seed, it too will grow and become huge. It will grow in your heart and grow in your life and grow in the world. And just as the mustard tree shelters birds, so God's kingdom will shelter people. But you must plant the seed.

The woman looked at Jesus again. She had the feeling that this was something she needed to know, but she just couldn't spare the time. 'I'm off,' she whispered to her friend. 'I'll see you later. If you get to understand how the kingdom of heaven applies to me, explain it to me this evening. But I'd better go and get the bread made.' Reluctantly, she stood up and turned to look one last time at Jesus the teacher. Just as she did so, Jesus caught her eye. He could see she wanted to stay, but he understood that she had much work to do at home.

'The kingdom of heaven,' he said, looking straight at her, 'is like this. A woman takes some yeast and mixes it with forty litres of flour until the whole batch of dough rises.' And he smiled at her. The woman looked back at Jesus and slowly considered what Jesus said. Suddenly, she smiled.

'I get it!' she said. 'I understand!' And she laughed.

'Well, I don't get it,' said her friend grumpily.

'Of course you do,' she said, turning to her friend excitedly. 'Jesus is saying that the kingdom of heaven works in the world like yeast works when you make bread. Flour on its own is just flour. You can add water and warm it, but nothing will happen. But when you add a little yeast and rub it through the flour, then the yeast starts to work and suddenly the whole lot changes and grows.

'Well, put God into your life and mix him in so that he spreads all through your life, and suddenly God's kingdom starts to grow. It expands in you and through you into the world. You can hardly see yeast in flour, and when it's mixed into the dough you can't see it at all, but it's so powerful that it changes everything. Put yeast in the flour and it changes the whole bread mix—put God in your heart and he changes your whole life. He brings it alive!

'It's like that mustard seed Jesus was talking about. The seed is small but it grows to be enormous. I think Jesus is telling us that the kingdom of heaven starts small but will get to be enormous. If we accept his teaching, we can change the world.

'But we have to do something first,' the woman said excitedly to her friend. 'We have to accept the teaching of Jesus and put it into our hearts. It's like we have to mix the yeast into our lives, or plant the mustard seed in our heart. Because if there is nothing planted, nothing can grow.

'Quick,' she said, pulling her friend to her feet. 'Let's get back home. We've got work to do!'

'What, bread making?' asked her friend.

'No! Kingdom making!' said the woman. And together they ran off to tell their friends all that they had learned.

BEGIN WITH AN ATTITUDE OF GRATITUDE

Start by being thankful for all the good things that came out of last week's circle time. Use this time to refer to, and critically review, successes recorded on the noticeboard. Refer to particular children and any successes they may have had, and note any other good outcomes from last week's circle time.

BIBLE STORY SUMMARY

The yeast in the dough

This is a difficult story! But it could be summarized like this. Just as yeast works in flour, causing it to change for the better and grow, so God's kingdom works in the world, causing it to change for the better and grow. You can't see God's kingdom but you can see its results.

GET STARTED

Recipe for a good school

Fold, and then tear, A4 paper into eight pieces. Each piece will be about 10cm x 7cm. Give each child in the circle a piece of the paper. Ask them to write their name on the paper and then write several things that they feel makes your school a good place. Ask them to be specific—for example, a particular playground game, a lesson they enjoy, a favourite area of the school, a club they like, even a lunchtime supervisor or teacher whom they love. Then ask them all to go and hide the paper somewhere in the classroom.

Return everyone to their seats and explain that these good things all go into the mixture that makes your school a wonderful place. Explain that these things are always there, making the school a good place, even though we don't always notice them. Like the yeast, they are sometimes unnoticed. Then ask the children to go off again and find a piece of paper that is not their own. As soon as they have found one, they are to come back to their seat.

GET REAL

Go around the circle with each child reading out one thing from the piece of paper, starting with the words, 'One ingredient that makes this school good is…'

GET RIGHT

What would Jesus want us to do? He would want us to be our best selves.

So which of God's guidelines is relevant to this circle?

> All of them! If we live by the guidelines, we help to make the school into the best place that it can be—we bake good bread. When we don't live by the guidelines—when we argue, lie or boast, for example—we spoil the school.

GET TOGETHER

Photocopy the recipe sheet opposite, and ask the children to fill in the blanks with the things that they feel make your school the good place it is. Have a time of discussion first to help children to think about what makes a good school.

The following sample recipe sheet is a real example, completed by a girl called Amy.

Recipe for a good school.

Take a big mixing bowl and fill it with… Good children.

Pour in half a jug of… Snakes and ladders in the playground.

Add a pinch of… Head teacher.

Stir in a tablespoon of… *Goodnight Mr Tom*.

Mix with lots of… Computers.

Blend in some… PE lessons.

Knead with… Kind teachers… to make it smooth.

Season with… Mary, our school cook… to add some flavour.

Pour into… The 'Terrific Book'.

Sprinkle with… Yoga club… for decoration.

Cook until… 3.00pm.

Enjoy your school!

KEEP GOING

This week's noticeboard

Make a display of the children's recipes. You could place a table under the noticeboard, holding various packets, bottles and boxes, labelled appropriately. You might have a bottle labelled 'Sparkling Lessons', an empty box labelled 'Kind Friends', and so on. Provide some blank recipe sheets for the children to fill in, and some unlabelled packets and boxes that could be labelled as children notice good things throughout the week.

(Thanks to Perdy Buchanan-Barrow from Alexandra School, Harrow, for the idea of the recipe sheet and how to display it.)

KEEP IT IN MIND

Saying of the week

A good life can be a piece of cake!

Recipe for a Good School

Take a big mixing bowl and fill it with… _____

Pour in half a jug of… _____

Add a pinch of… _____

Stir in a tablespoon of… _____

Mix with lots of… _____

Blend in some… _____

Knead with… _____ to make it smooth.

Season with… _____ to add some flavour.

Pour into… _____

Sprinkle with… _____ for decoration.

Cook until… _____

Enjoy your school!

Reproduced with permission from *Stay Cool in School* published by BRF 2003 (1 84101 323 4)

IF YOU CAN'T SAY SOMETHIN' NICE, DON'T SAY NOTHIN' AT ALL

Don't condemn others, and God won't condemn you. God will be as hard on you as you are on others! He will treat you exactly as you treat them.

MATTHEW 7:1–2

GOD'S GUIDELINE

Be aware of your own faults but never judge or criticize other people.

○ ○ ● ✝ ○ ● ○

ZACCHAEUS THE TAX COLLECTOR

Jesus was going through Jericho, where a man named Zacchaeus lived. He was in charge of collecting taxes and was very rich. Jesus was heading his way, and Zacchaeus wanted to see what he was like. But Zacchaeus was a short man and could not see over the crowd. So he ran ahead and climbed up into a sycamore tree.

When Jesus got there, he looked up and said,

'Zacchaeus, hurry down! I want to stay with you today.' Zacchaeus hurried down and gladly welcomed Jesus.

Everyone who saw this started grumbling, 'This man Zacchaeus is a sinner! And Jesus is going home to eat with him.'

Later that day Zacchaeus stood up and said to the Lord, 'I will give half of my property to the poor. And I will now pay back four times as much to everyone I have ever cheated.'

Jesus said to Zacchaeus, 'Today you and your family have been saved, because you are a true son of Abraham. The Son of Man came to look for and to save people who are lost.'

LUKE 19:1–10

It was time for the Feast of the Passover and Jesus was travelling to Jerusalem with his disciples. As the disciples travelled along, they were talking and enjoying each other's company. When they arrived in the town of Jericho, hundreds of people came to find them. They all wanted to hear Jesus, the great teacher, speak. Many people had heard that he could work miracles and heal people, and they flocked to the road so that they might catch a glimpse of him and maybe even hear him speak.

The crowd grew and grew as one friend told another of the arrival of Jesus and together they hurried down to find a place where they would be able to see Jesus pass by.

But one man had no friends to keep a place for him at the front of the crowd. That man was called Zacchaeus. Zacchaeus was not a popular man—he was a tax collector. That meant he worked for the hated Romans, the occupying army. He collected the tax money from the people in Jericho and gave it to the Romans. But being shunned and hated for his job had not improved Zacchaeus' character. Not only did he collect the taxes (which was unpopular but legal), but he also stole money from his fellow Jews. He took extra money from them, on top of the tax they owed, and kept it for himself. People knew that he did this and so he was hated even more.

So on the day that Jesus came to Jericho, Zacchaeus had no one to save him a place by the side of the road. To make things worse, Zacchaeus was a short man, and when he found himself pushed to the back of the crowd, he could not see anything at all. He knew that if he was to be able to see Jesus he would have to take desperate measures! Looking around him, he could see nothing. Then, something made him look up. There was his answer. A sturdy sycamore tree was just above him, and if he could only climb into the tree he would be able to see the great man Jesus.

What was it that made Zacchaeus so anxious to see Jesus? Did he somehow know that Jesus was the only person who could help him become his best self again? No one knows. But we do know that he was so desperate to see Jesus that he put his dignity aside and scrambled up the tree like a boy. And there he sat, waiting for Jesus to come by.

No one noticed the unpopular Zacchaeus sitting up on his perch in the tree. They were all too busy cheering Jesus as he came along the road. But Jesus saw him. He looked up into the tree and saw Zacchaeus. He did not see the same Zacchaeus that everyone else saw, though. He saw the man Zacchaeus could be, if only he turned away from doing wicked things.

What do you think Jesus said to Zacchaeus to get him to stop being a bad man? Did he shout at him and tell him off for being bad? No. Did he pull him out of the tree and laugh at him in front of his friends and neighbours? No. Did he reject Zacchaeus and tell him to get out of his sight, for he was such a bad person? No.

Do you know what Jesus did? He called out to him, 'Zacchaeus, hurry and come down. I must stay at your house today!' Isn't that amazing? Jesus said, 'Come here, Zacchaeus, and I will be your friend.' And off he went to Zacchaeus' house to have supper with him.

Well, all the people were furious. How could Jesus possibly be friends with someone who was so bad? Jesus shouldn't like Zacchaeus. He should be horrible to him, he should reject him as we do, they all said. But later, after supper, Zacchaeus was a changed man. He went and apologized to the people he had swindled. He stood in front of them and said, 'I will give half of all my possessions to the poor. And if I have cheated anyone I will pay back four times more.'

With those words, everyone realized that Jesus had worked another miracle—he had turned Zacchaeus into a good, honest man. How had he done it? They waited to hear what Jesus would say. He turned to the crowd and said, 'Zacchaeus has been saved today. This is why I came, to find people who are lost, people just like Zacchaeus, and bring them back to God.' And how had he helped Zacchaeus to be his best self again? Not by shouting, punishing, humiliating, embarrassing or rejecting him. No, he did it by being kind to him and accepting him. He did it by being a loving friend.

BEGIN WITH AN ATTITUDE OF GRATITUDE

Look at the noticeboard for children's successes following the previous week's circle time. Use these as prompts for a time of thanks. As well as having a time of thanks for these successes, it is a good idea to note down during the week any other successes the children may have had from ideas from other circle times, even from several weeks before.

BIBLE STORY SUMMARY

Zacchaeus the tax collector

Do you remember that Zacchaeus was a bit of a Norman No-Mates? This was because he not only collected taxes from his own people to give to the

Romans, who were the occupying army, but he also swindled his neighbours. Naturally this did not make Zacchaeus very popular. But when Jesus saw Zacchaeus, he did not judge him or even mention his faults. He just accepted him and offered him loving friendship. This love overwhelmed Zacchaeus and he changed his mind and made amends.

GET STARTED

Quickly muddle the children up with a 'cross-the-circle' game. For example, cross the circle if…

- You like fish.
- You own a dog.
- You like cold custard.
- You get sick in cars.
- You remember POGS.
- Your mum sings in the car.

When the children are muddled up, you can play the game 'Common ground'. Put the children into pairs around the circle and get each pair to talk together and find two things that they both like. These might be things they like to do, to eat, to play, to visit, to wear, to listen to or to watch.

Once they have had time to chat (two or three minutes at most), go around the circle saying, 'This is my friend… (*name*) and we both like…' Each child in the pair names the other child and one thing they have discovered that they both like. This means that every child in the circle will speak.

GET REAL

In the story, Jesus said, 'This is my friend Zacchaeus and we both like eating supper. Come down, Zacchaeus. I am your friend.' Because everyone else was hostile and horrible to Zacchaeus, he never changed his ways. But Jesus just offered unconditional friendship. This melted Zacchaeus' heart and he apologized and even gave money back to the people he had robbed. By his kindness Jesus helped Zacchaeus to be his best self.

Remind the children that everyone knows what it's like to feel a bit unhappy or lonely or left out in school. Ask the children to sit silently for twenty seconds and think about a specific time when they felt either lonely or left out of things. Ask the children to go around the circle with the sentence 'I felt a bit lonely in school when…' or 'I felt a bit left out when…' (Remind them that they are not to mention another child's name in a derogatory way.)

GET RIGHT

Encourage the children to discuss some of the reasons they have given for feeling left out or lonely. These reasons may be to do with being judged hopeless at something and so not being included; or friends re-forming friendship groups and excluding them, so that they felt left out and judged unworthy of a place in the group; or being new to a group.

What would Jesus want us to do? What do God's guidelines say?

> Be aware of your own faults but never judge or criticize other people.

If we look at God's guidelines, we can see what Jesus would do. He would say that we should not judge or criticize each other. We should just be kind and loving towards each other. When people are kind and accepting towards you, it helps you to be your best self.

GET TOGETHER

This week we need to think about how we can be kind and accepting towards each other. Encourage a discussion about the best ways to be kind to one another. Ask the children for their suggestions. These might include:

- Notice the good things people do and say 'thank you' to them.
- Make kind offers to people we don't usually talk to. For example, 'Would you like to work in my group?'
- Quickly offer to be a partner in PE to someone who is left on their own.
- Don't fuss about who we sit next to in circle time.
- Be careful not to either gossip or pass on gossip.
- Don't say people are rubbish at football (even if they are!)
- Co-operate with people we don't know too well. For example, set up games in the playground with them.
- Never call anyone fat or skinny or 'Ging-er' or any other unkind and thoughtless name.
- Remember that if people say sorry to us we should forgive them quickly.

KEEP GOING

This week's noticeboard

This week's noticeboard title is 'Come on down!'

Photocopy the tree template on page 102, and several small 'Zacchaeus' figures (opposite). Pin the

• Occupying younger children with songs or games or pencil-and-paper activities during a wet playtime.
• Asking an unfamiliar child to join in a game.

If you have no camera, the children could write about what they have done and pin their accounts to the noticeboard.

KEEP IT IN MIND

Saying of the week

Stone beats scissors
But 'kind' beats 'cross'.
It's better to be friends
Than trying to be the boss!

tree to the noticeboard, with the Zacchaeus figures in a pocket in the 'branches' of the tree.

Explain to the children that they are going to have a whole week where they are kind to each other and do not judge each other. Jesus was kind to Zacchaeus and did not judge him.

If you have a digital camera, you could make a display of digital photographs of the children in your class co-operating with others who are not necessarily their best friends. You have to be consciously kind to work successfully with unfamiliar people. Whenever the children are photographed working with others, they can take a 'Zacchaeus' out of the tree and pin him to the board underneath the tree and next to their photo.

Co-operative activities might include:

• Tidying the school library.
• Organizing playground games for younger children.
• Tidying up a messy area of school.
• Cleaning out a pet's cage together.
• Working in unfamiliar groups in lessons.

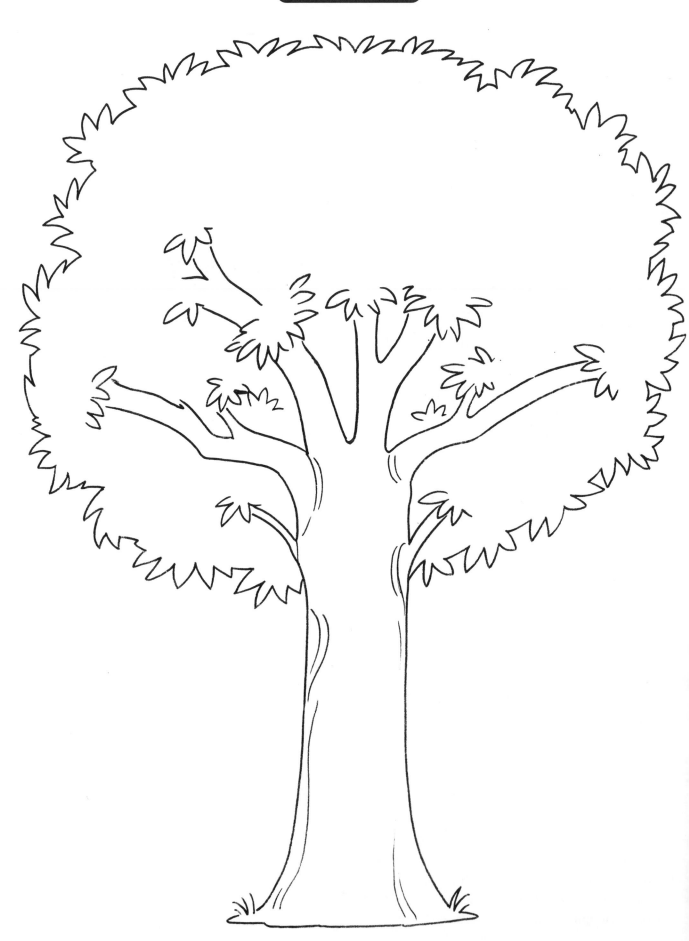

Reproduced with permission from *Stay Cool in School* published by BRF 2003 (1 84101 323 4)

RUB IT OUT, DON'T RUB IT IN

If you forgive others for the wrongs they do to you, your Father in heaven will forgive you. But if you don't forgive others, your Father will not forgive your sins.

MATTHEW 6:14–15

You know that our ancestors were told, 'Do not murder' and 'A murderer must be brought to trial.' But I promise you that if you are angry with someone, you will have to stand trial.

MATTHEW 5:21–22

Don't condemn others, and God won't condemn you. God will be as hard on you as you are on others! He will treat you exactly as you treat them.

MATTHEW 7:1–2

—∘∘● GOD'S GUIDELINES ●∘∘—

Be loving and forgiving to all people, even to those you really don't like and who don't like you.

Stay calm, do not be angry with each other, never take revenge and never try to get your own back or get even.

—∘∘● ●∘∘—

THE PARABLE OF THE UNFORGIVING MAN

Peter came up to the Lord and asked, 'How many times should I forgive someone who does something wrong to me? Is seven times enough?' Jesus answered:

Not just seven times, but seventy-seven times! This story will show you what the kingdom of heaven is like:

One day a king decided to call in his officials and ask them to give an account of what they owed him. As he was doing this, one official was brought in who owed him fifty million silver coins. But he didn't have any money to pay what he owed. The king ordered him to be sold, along with his wife and children and all he owned, in order to pay the debt.

The official got down on his knees and began begging, 'Have pity on me, and I will pay you every penny I owe!' The king felt sorry for him and let him go free. He even told the official that he did not have to pay back the money.

As the official was leaving, he happened to meet another official, who owed him a hundred silver coins. So he grabbed the man by the throat. He started choking him and said, 'Pay me what you owe.'

The man got down on his knees and began begging, 'Have pity on me, and I will pay you back.' But the first official refused to have pity. Instead, he went and had the other official put in jail until he could pay what he owed.

When some other officials found out what had happened, they felt sorry for the man who had been put in jail. Then they told the king what had happened. The king called the first official back in and said, 'You're an evil man! When you begged for mercy, I said you did not have to pay back a penny. Don't you think you should show pity to someone else, as I did to you?' The king was so angry that he ordered the official to be tortured until he could pay back everything he owed. That is how my Father in heaven will treat you, if you don't forgive each of my followers with all your heart.

MATTHEW 18:21–35

One of the most important lessons Jesus taught was how important it is that we forgive each other. Forgiveness is not an easy thing! Jesus said that we are to forgive people who upset us or even do us harm. What is more, we have to forgive them even if they don't ask to be forgiven, don't want to be forgiven or don't even accept they have done anything wrong! Now that's really hard. It means that if someone is horrid to you, you have to forgive them—completely—even if they don't say sorry, and even if they are *not* sorry. That's asking a lot, isn't it? But Jesus says, in many different stories and teaching, that we have to forgive others.

When Jesus was crucified (which means being nailed alive to a piece of wood and left to die in the hot sun), one of the last things he did was to ask God to forgive the people who had done this to him. Jesus never asked anyone to do anything he was not prepared to do himself. Christians believe that Jesus died on the cross as a way of paying off the debt we all owe God for all the bad things we have done.

It took a while for even the disciples of Jesus to understand how serious Jesus really was about the importance of forgiving each other. One day, Peter asked Jesus yet another question about forgiveness. This one was about exactly how many times he was supposed to forgive someone who had upset him. He said, 'If I forgive someone seven times, will that do?' Jesus looked at him. 'No, Peter, that will not do. Try seventy-seven times.' Peter thought about this. Seventy-seven times! Even the most annoying person he knew did not upset him that often. That must mean Jesus was telling him he had to forgive people for every wrong they ever did to him. This was a tough teaching. 'Why?' he asked. 'Why do I have to be that nice? Why have I got to be so forgiving?' 'I will explain,' said Jesus. And he told this story.

Once, there was a king who decided to check the accounts of his workers. He had just started when a servant was brought in who owed him millions of pounds—literally millions. 'Can you even begin to pay this debt?' he asked the man. And when the man said 'No', he said, 'Right. I am going to sell you as a slave, along with your wife and your children. Then I am going to sell everything you own and keep the money to help pay off this enormous amount of money you owe me.' (This would have been usual in Jesus' time.)

The man fell on his knees before the king and pleaded with him. 'Oh please,' begged the man, 'please, give me some time. I will pay you everything.' The king looked at the man and he felt truly sorry for him. 'I have decided to forgive you the entire debt. You no longer owe me any money. You are free to go home to your wife and family, and you can keep your home.' The man left the king's room.

A few minutes later, however, the man bumped into a fellow servant who owed him some money—not much, just a couple of pounds. 'Oi, you,' he said to this man. 'You owe me money!' And he got him by the throat and started choking him. 'You pay me what you owe me, now!' he yelled. 'Oh please,' begged the man, 'please, give me some time. I will pay you everything.' But he refused and instead had the fellow servant taken away from his family and thrown into jail until he should pay the debt.

Now the king got to hear about this and he was furious. He called the first man to him. 'You evil man!' he said. 'I forgave you the whole amount you owed me, just because you asked me to. You should have forgiven your fellow servant just as I forgave you. Right, you can go to jail until you can pay me back all of the millions of pounds you owe me.' (And that would have been for ever.) 'That,' said Jesus, 'is how God will treat each one of you unless you forgive each other from your heart.'

BEGIN WITH AN ATTITUDE OF GRATITUDE

Look at last week's noticeboard and praise the children for their successes. Note any particular successes.

BIBLE STORY SUMMARY

The unforgiving man

This week's story was about a man who owed the king millions of pounds. He asked the king if he could have time to pay. But the king was a generous man and said that he did not have to pay anything. Out of love, and the kindness of his heart, he forgave the debt entirely. However, this same man was owed a few pounds by another servant, and he would not forgive that debt. Instead he had the man thrown into jail until he could pay. The king heard about this and was furious. 'I forgave you so much, but you can't forgive another person even a little. Now I am going

to throw you into jail. Get out of my sight until the whole debt you owed me is paid.'

In this story Jesus was trying to explain how God will forgive our sins if we ask him to—he will forgive us everything. But we have to do the same for other people. God has forgiven us so much—all he asks is that we forgive each other.

GET STARTED

Cross the circle if you have ever…

- Been annoyed with someone for taking something without asking you.
- Shouted at a brother or sister because they turned the TV over while you were watching a programme.
- Felt angry because people laughed at you in PE.
- Been furious because someone took your best friend away from you.
- Felt angry because your 'friends' wouldn't let you play football.
- Been hurt and angry because you discovered people had talked about you behind your back.
- Been really upset because you were the only one of a group who was not invited to a party.
- Been really mad at a teacher because they made you look a fool in front of the whole class.

Add any other examples of understandable anger that you can think of.

GET REAL

Go around the circle, using 'Forgiving people is hard because…' as the opening part of the sentence. Be sure you give the group twenty seconds' silent thinking time before you start the 'go-around'.

GET RIGHT

What would Jesus want us to do in these circumstances? In the story, he said we have to forgive each other. He didn't really imply that there was an option! Which of God's guidelines is relevant here? Well, several of them—but we will be thinking about two of them in particular.

> Be loving and forgiving to all people, even to those you really don't like and who don't like you.
>
> Stay calm, do not be angry with each other, never take revenge and never try to get your own back or get even.

In the story of the unforgiving man, Jesus said that God forgives us our huge sins and faults, and we have to forgive those who have sinned against us—not grip them by the throat as did the man in the story! If someone has upset us in any way we are to forgive them. Just that—forgive them. In the prayer Jesus taught his disciples, he told them to say, 'Forgive us our sins *as* we forgive those who sin against us.' In other words you will only be forgiven if you forgive. That 'as' is pretty important! It implies an equation in which our being forgiven is dependent upon us forgiving others.

GET TOGETHER

As we saw in the round, forgiving is difficult. We often want to get back at people, get cross or get even. Sometimes when we do those things we feel better. It can give us a temporary feeling of pleasure to see someone suffer in the way we have done. But that is

wrong. One of God's guidelines is called 'the Golden Rule'. It is found in Matthew 7:12. Jesus says that this is the whole sum of the Law of Moses: 'Always treat others as you would like them to treat you.'

That is the real Golden Rule. All other rules or moral values are just a way of helping us to understand and do this one. Have a general discussion about why forgiving others is such a difficult thing to do. You will then need to ask the children to think of ways in which they can forgive others. I would suggest something like this.

First ask the children to think of situations in which forgiveness is needed to make the situations right again. Write them down as the children think of them. (Don't let the children mention actual names.) They might be such things as were mentioned in the cross-the-circle game, but the children will also have their own suggestions.

Now ask them to think of ways they could act to show that they had stopped blaming or holding grudges. For example, smiling at the person who had upset you, asking them to play a game, sharing your crisps with them, sitting next to them at lunchtime and being pleasant, and so on. Write down all the ideas, but don't forget—no actual names!

KEEP GOING

This week's noticeboard
This idea is to help children to see a visual representation of forgiveness as a movement from the darkness of blame and anger into the brightness of peace and forgiveness.

Cover the noticeboard in blue backing paper, and paint a large, radiant sun in the middle of the board. Make sure the sun is huge and bright. You could put some silver paint in with the yellow, gold and orange. Paint rays shining out from the sun, almost to the edges of the board.

Give each child a piece of black sugar paper, or something similar. This should be about A4 size if you

can afford it, slightly smaller if not. Ask the children to write about something that has upset them recently. Tell them that they can use the example they gave during the 'Get together' section. They can write everything that happened and why it has made them upset. They must not mention names, though. Better to write, 'I was the only girl in our group who was not invited to a birthday party. Everyone went ice-skating. I would have loved it', rather than 'Emily left me out of her birthday party. She invited every-one else ice-skating.'

As the paper is black, it is best to write in pencil.

Ask them to fold the paper in two and write their name on the outside in pencil. Collect in the papers and staple them closed so that they cannot be casu-ally read. Pin the black notes all over the noticeboard. Aim to cover the sun completely and as much of the sky as you can. If possible, cover the entire notice-board so that it appears blacked out.

Explain to the children that they are going to try to act in a forgiving way this week towards whoever has upset them as described in the note. When they have done this, and have made a good effort at forgiveness, they may remove their black note from the board. Put a cardboard box with a slot in it below the notice-board, ready to receive the used notes. Explain that as the week progresses and people forgive each other, the noticeboard will go from black to bright sunlight. When you live with blame and anger and unforgive-ness, you live in the darkness, but when you forgive each other you can live in the light of love.

KEEP IT IN MIND

Saying of the week

Forgive and God forgets.

GAMES APPENDIX

These are the games that appear in the book. They are reproduced here so that you can photocopy them and re-use them for other circle times you may run.

TRAFFIC LIGHTS

Ask all the children to stand in the middle of the circle. Explain that you are going to ask them what they would do as part of a group in various scenarios. Your left-hand side of the circle is 'red light'. This is the side for 'No'. Your right-hand side of the circle is 'green light'. This is the side for 'Yes'.

Read out each of the scenarios. The children must decide on their response and run to the 'red light' or 'green light' on the word 'Go'.

After playing the game, put the class into groups of about six pupils each. Have the scenario cards on pages 28–30 photocopied before the lesson, and give one card to each group. Ask them to act out the scenario, perhaps once with one ending and then with a different ending.

TRUST TRAIN

Move a few chairs away from the circle so that there are 'holes' in the circle.

Put the children into teams of five, and ask each team to stand in a queue. Now ask the children to put their hands on the shoulders of the person in front of them. Explain that they are a train. The person at the back is the driver; the person at the front is the engine. The engine will go where the driver tells it to go.

If the driver taps with their left hand on the left shoulder of the person in front of them, that person has to pass the tap along to the next person, and so on down the line to the engine—who turns left.

Passing down a right-hand tap on the right shoulder turns the engine right. Passing down a tap on both shoulders means 'go straight on'. Passing down a gentle pull on both the shoulders, with both hands, means the engine stops. There is no reverse!

Get everybody to practise tapping and passing along the taps really efficiently. Then tell everybody that their trains are now about to set off around the room—but there is one further instruction. Everybody, apart from the driver at the back, must have their eyes tightly closed. This is scary for the engine at the front. This is why the game is called 'Trust train'!

GETTING TO KNOW YOU.

Sit all the children in the circle and explain to them that they must follow your instructions:

- All stand up and generally mill around the circle. (This must be done in silence.)
- Stop.
- Say hello to everyone you pass.
- Walk.
- Stop.
- Give a 'high five' to the next six people you pass.
- Walk.
- Stop.
- Make a group of four.
- Ask each other the question, 'If you could invite anyone into this room, who would it be?'
- Split up and mill around the room again in silence.
- Make a group of three.
- Tell each other about the last time you can remember being scared.
- Walk.
- Stop.
- Turn to the person next to you.
- Label yourselves 'A' and 'B'.

- Tell each other which piece of music or song always makes you feel cheerful.
- 'B' close your eyes tight.
- 'A' take 'B's hand and lead them back to a chair in the circle. Carefully shield them from any harm as you lead them back.
- Sit down next to them.

COMMON GROUND

To play this, you need to go around the circle putting the children into pairs.

Then you give them one-and-a-half minutes to talk to each other. They have to find two things they have in common—for example, hobbies, holidays, pets, favourite lessons, food and so on. After this, you go around the circle and each child introduces their partner with the words, 'This is my friend… (name) … and we both…'. Each person in the pair says one of the things they both have in common. For example:

Richard: 'This is my friend Rachael and we both like watching *The Simpsons*.'

Rachael: 'This is my friend Richard and we both like holidays in Swanage.'

This activity helps us to see that we have more things in common with each other than we may have previously realized.

SHOAL OF CARP ON THE CENTRAL LINE

Go around the circle putting the children into pairs. Ask the pairs to label themselves 'A' and 'B'.

This game is about excuses. For two minutes 'A' has to ask 'B' lots of questions about why certain things have not been done or completed. 'B' has to give an excuse each time. Sometimes, 'B' can give a completely mad excuse just to liven up the game! (The title of the game comes from a real incident when a furious director asked one of my fellow students at drama school why he was late for a rehearsal. With a charming smile the friend replied, 'So sorry. Train delayed—shoal of carp on the Central Line.') After

two minutes, swap over so that 'B' asks 'A' questions.

If the class is struggling to invent questions, put a long list on the board or a flipchart. For example:

- Where is your reading book?
- Why didn't you tidy your room last night?
- Where is your PE kit?
- Did you go to your swimming lesson this week?
- Why did you argue back with your mum?
- Why haven't you done your maths homework?
- Why didn't you learn your spellings for the test this week?
- Why didn't you come to see me at break as I asked you to?
- Why didn't you set the table as you were asked to do?
- Why didn't you practise your piano/recorder/ underwater basket-weaving (as appropriate)?
- Why didn't you go and see your grandma as you promised?
- Why didn't you water the plants in the classroom when you said you would?

TIME-LIMITED ZOOM AND EEK

The only way to win this game is to put others before yourself. The object of the game is to go right around the circle with each child having said the word 'zoom' within a given time limit, usually one minute. To make it difficult, each child is also allowed to say 'eek' just once. If they say 'eek', they reverse the direction of the zoom.

The difficulty is this: it is good fun to take control of the game and say 'eek', but if you do so near the end of the game, it may not be possible to get the 'zoom' back to the beginning of the circle within the minute! Children therefore have to balance their desire to say 'eek', take control of the game and reverse the direction of the 'zoom', with their desire to have a group success and get the 'zoom' back to the beginning of the circle within the minute. The group's desire to 'win' may pressurize them into forgoing their desire to say 'eek'.

CROSS-THE-CIRCLE

This game is infinitely variable and deceptively simple. It has several aims. First of all, it is designed to move the children around so that they are not permanently parked next to their best friend. When children sit next to their best friends they often adopt similar attitudes and opinions. It is desirable to encourage children to think for themselves—which is one of the few ways we will ever counter the effect of peer pressure.

Second, the game helps children to realize that they are not the only person to have certain problems, difficulties or weaknesses. This can be very helpful. If you say, for example, 'Cross the circle if you sometimes lose your temper at home,' and several children cross the circle, it can help a child to feel able to acknowledge that they too have a problem with controlling their temper. It's a great deal easier to sort out your problems if you aren't labouring under the misapprehension that you are the worst, the weirdest or the dumbest person in the class!

Lastly, the basic thesis of this book is that we cannot get to grips with our problems if we won't first learn to be honest with ourselves. 'Cross-the-circle' games can help us to be honest with ourselves.

Some examples of 'Cross-the-circle' in this book are:

Be honest!

This game is designed to encourage children to be honest with themselves. Cross the circle if you have ever:

- Looked at a pile of wet towels on the bathroom floor, thought, 'Someone else will pick them up' and left the room.
- Borrowed something without asking.
- Eaten the last biscuit in the tin.
- Borrowed something and not given it back.
- Made a face behind someone's back.
- Been a bit of a show-off.
- 'Forgotten' to give your mum or dad the change.
- Said you were ill when you wanted to get out of doing something.
- Been a bit too keen to tell everyone how good you are at PlayStation.
- Said you'd do something and then 'forgotten'—like walking the dog/cleaning out the rabbit/feeding the fish.
- Eaten biscuits or crisps in your bedroom and then stuffed the wrappers or bags under your bed.
- Kicked your brother or sister under the table.
- Told everyone how nice you had been to a new girl.
- Boasted about all the things you can do on your skateboard.
- Quietly left the kitchen when it was time to clear the table or do the washing-up.
- Deliberately got your brother or sister into trouble by telling on them.
- Let everyone one know how well you did in your ballet exam.
- Told your mum you had tidied your room when really all you had done was to pick up all the clothes from the floor and dump them in the dirty laundry basket.

Use as many or as few of these suggestions as you choose. The aim is to make sure everyone in the group moves at least once, so invent other age-appropriate examples. Include light-hearted examples of common childhood dishonesty, idleness or pride as well as more serious things.

By the end, everyone should have moved. If not, finish with, 'Cross the circle if you have ever told a fib—even a very little one.'

Say to the class, 'Well done! It's great to know I have a really honest class. Nobody, but nobody, is perfect!'

Apologies

Cross the circle if you have ever:

- Upset anyone (That should be everyone!)
- Thought 'I'm not going to be the first to say sorry.'
- Found it hard to think how to say sorry.
- Been mean to someone who is trying to say sorry.
- Said sorry and then spoiled it by saying 'But...' as in 'I am sorry I called you a wally, but you shouldn't have said my shoes were naff yesterday.'

Materialism

Cross the circle if:

- You are currently saving up for something.
- You dislike anyone touching your possessions.
- You spend lots of time planning what you are going to buy.
- You sometimes feel jealous of other people's possessions.
- You sometimes find it difficult to share your possessions.

If you have enjoyed this book and would like further information regarding circle time, INSET and other training for your school, please contact:

Margaret Goldthorpe
'Stay Cool in School'
Midsummer Cottage
Moor Lane
Sarratt
Herts
WD3 6BY
Tel: 01923 262586